Lisa Doodson, PhD, is one of the UK's foremost experts in the field of stepfamilies and currently works as a lecturer in psychology at Thames Valley University. She writes for national magazines and press on the topic of extended families and relationships, helping people understand the pressures of stepfamily living and offering advice on dealing with difficulties within their families.

Contents

Acknowledgements

I wouldn't have been able to carry out my research or write this book without the help and support of all the stepfamilies who gave up their time so willingly and generously to share their experiences with me. I'd like to take the opportunity to thank them and wish them all the very best for their families in the future.

To my agents Jaine and Antony, who were brave enough to recognise the need for this book and helped me nurture and develop my ideas, I'm eternally grateful.

I'd like to thank my editor, Julia Kellaway, who is always such a joy to work with. I'm so grateful for her belief in the book and her continued patience, professionalism and skill in keeping me on track throughout the project.

And finally, I'd like to thank my husband, Mike, for always encouraging and supporting me in whatever I do; and to my children, Helena, Alex and Liam, for making me so proud to be their mum and stepmum.

Introduction

As a stepmother and psychologist, I have written this book to help women understand the common problems faced by stepmothers and how to cope effectively with adjusting to life in a stepfamily.

I became interested in the psychology of stepfamilies after becoming a stepmother myself when I met my partner 10 years ago. At the time, he had a young son aged two while I had two children, a six-year-old daughter and a son aged three. Although we'd spent time talking about how everything would work in principle, in practice things were very different. I was shocked by how hard I found it to adjust to stepfamily life. One day I'd be on cloud nine thinking how lucky I was to have such a wonderful new family: a fantastically caring husband, two happy children of my own and a new stepson. The next day, I'd be inconsolable, frustrated by the fact we weren't a 'normal' family and never would be. Every little thing that made us 'different' from other families in my eyes made me sad and yearn for something we could never be. I'm normally a 'glass half full' type of girl but the pressures of stepfamily life were testing my optimism. My husband, on the other hand, seemed to take to his twin roles as stepfather and father like a duck to water. He saw the positive in everything we did. If we had the children with us, fantastic

– we could have a family day out. If we didn't, great – we could escape for an adult-only weekend. Why couldn't I be as positive?

I began to feel angry with myself for not being able to cope better so set out to look for help. Was it just me who felt like this or did other stepmums feel the same? Surely there were successful stepmums out there who could show me the ropes?

But when I started looking I was shocked by the lack of help for stepmothers. Although there has been quite a lot of research on stepfamilies in general, stepmothers seem to be the poor relation, with very little recent research. I decided to use my skills as a psychologist to understand more about the common issues women face when they become part of a stepfamily and help them identify ways of coping effectively with their problems.

When you first become part of a stepfamily you'd be forgiven for thinking that you were the first one in living memory. There are so few positive role models out there and rarely any good-news stories involving happy, successful stepfamilies. Even from childhood we're used to reading about the wicked stepmother in fairy stories and watching them in pantomimes every year at Christmas. No wonder that we sometimes struggle to see our stepfamily roles in a positive light. What you need to tell yourself is that you're not alone. Stepfamilies are actually the fastest-growing family type in the UK, with estimates suggesting that 1 in 10 of all families are now stepfamilies. This means that approximately 700,000 step-parents currently live with and raise their stepchildren. But that's not the whole story. The most recent

UK census only classifies a family as a stepfamily if there are *resident* stepchildren. So if you look after your stepchildren on a part-time basis, such as at weekends and holidays, you aren't included within these statistics. Given that the majority of stepmothers are 'part-time' step-parents this means that the overall number of stepmothers is probably closer to double the current estimates. So not only are we stepmothers part of an ever-growing population, we are also largely 'hidden' from any official figures. It's hard to know how many of us there actually are, let alone begin to offer us some support!

And it's not just the government that struggles with defining stepfamilies. If I stopped 10 people in the street and asked them to define a stepfamily I would probably get 10 different answers. For example, if you live with your partner and he has grown-up children from a previous relationship are you a stepmother? If your husband has a child from a previous relationship whom you have never met, are you a stepmother? Are you part of a stepfamily if the person you've been dating for the past year has children from another relationship? At what point do you become a stepmother or part of a stepfamily?

One stepmother I spoke to struggled with her status within her stepfamily. Heather had been in a relationship with her partner for over five years. He had a young daughter from a previous relationship. Heather enjoyed spending time with her stepdaughter and felt they had developed a really special bond. However, Heather struggled to be accepted by her stepdaughter's biological mother. Things came to a head when Heather's stepdaughter's birthday was approaching. Although Heather had helped her partner arrange the party she was told by her stepdaughter's mother that she couldn't attend. Heather was heartbroken. She really wanted to be part of the celebrations and watch her stepdaughter enjoy her party. However, when she turned to her best friend for some moral support, she was shocked by her friend's reaction. Heather's friend couldn't understand what the problem was as she reasoned that Heather wasn't even the stepmother given that her 'stepdaughter's' biological mother was still alive. Her friend believed that you could only be a stepparent on the death of the biological parent. Now while it's true to say that many years ago stepfamilies were usually created after the death of a parent that's far from the case now and I think few people would hold such an extreme view of stepfamilies. However, I think it does illustrate the point that the actual definition of a stepfamily is still far from clear in many people's minds.

If you look in most modern dictionaries, a stepmother is still defined as the 'wife of your father by a subsequent marriage'; however, most women would consider themselves a stepmother long before marriage, usually when they start to live with their partner or even when they start dating them seriously. If your partner has children from a previous relationship then you by default take on some form of stepparenting role. This is the case regardless of the amount of contact or the age of the children or whether you are married to or co-habiting with your partner.

To clarify, a 'stepmother' as referred to in this book is defined as when:

➤ you marry someone who has children from a
  previous relationship
➤ you co-habit with someone who has children
  from a previous relationship
➤ you have a long-standing relationship with
  someone who already has children
➤ your partner's children reside with you
  permanently
➤ your partner's children come to stay at
  weekends and holidays
➤ you don't see your partner's children any more
➤ you've never met your partner's children
➤ your partner's children are grown up

Try not to focus on the word 'stepmother' as this implies that you have some type of mothering role to your stepchildren – which may not be the case. Your 23-year-old stepdaughter is hardly likely to need you in the same way a toddler might! But if your partner has children – whatever their age or needs – you will be affected in some way, whether your stepchildren live with you, whether they are adults with children of their own or whether you barely see them. Even if you don't consider yourself a stepmother to your partner's children, you are just as likely to be faced with step-parenting challenges – to differing degrees – as all other stepmums.

Having scoured bookshops, websites and academic journals to try and understand the stepmother role, I became certain that stepmothers face unique problems. Stepmothers appeared to be finding it difficult to adapt to their role in the stepfamily and often felt they didn't get the support or help they needed from their family and friends to cope with the pressures of stepfamily life. I wanted to understand these difficulties in more detail and, more importantly, I wanted to know how they affect stepmothers' overall well-being. I wanted to talk to women who were 'new to the job' and those who had years of experience; those who became stepmothers when they were young, and those who found themselves with a new step-family when they were not so young; those with young stepchildren and those who inherited the grown-up versions. And I especially wanted to talk to women who had been through the problems and emerged from the other side, so that they could become the role models for other stepmothers embarking on their journey.

The stepmothers who took part in the research were fantastic in their openness, honesty and willingness to help others. Having spent many years learning how to be a stepmum – sometimes taking the scenic route! – they were eager to help others avoid the same pitfalls they had encountered. They wanted to share their experiences of what had worked for them in becoming happier, contented step-mothers. Pam's email was typical of many I received.

I am a part-time stepmother to four children and mother to two. When I first became a stepmother (about six years ago) I read a lot around the area but was disappointed to find most of the literature came from the States rather than the UK and so was at times difficult to relate to. I am delighted to know there is now proper research being conducted in the UK on stepfamilies and wish it had been conducted in time for me to learn from it! The role as a stepmum is so hard to fulfil because of its ambiguity. There don't seem to be any set boundaries or etiquette and everyone in the new family seems to have such different expectations.

PAM, STEPMUM FOR SIX YEARS TO FOUR STEPCHILDREN
AGED FROM 9 TO 15

Other women spoke of the difficulties they had in taking on the role 'full-time', where the stark differences between their previous single life and new family life proved hard to adjust to. As Sarah explained:

I am a 34-year-old stepmother and my stepdaughter is now 22. She was nine years old when I first moved in with my husband to be. Aged 22 I had to learn how to run a house, work, be a partner and then suddenly a step-parent too. There were many tears, mainly more from me than my stepdaughter, but we got there...finally...and we love each other so much now that the word 'step' seems to make us more distant and unloving than we really are.

SARAH, STEPMUM FOR 13 YEARS TO 22-YEAR-OLD
STEPDAUGHTER

In the course of my research for the book I interviewed over 250 stepmothers – the largest study of stepmothers undertaken in the UK. The women I talked to gave me unique insights into the difficulties and challenges they faced with their new role as stepmum.

What I came to realise, both through my own experiences and through talking to others, is that it takes time and practice to become good at step-parenting, just like anything worthwhile in life. Everyone needs a bit of instruction as well as lots of encouragement when they start out learning something new, whether it's playing an instrument, learning to ride a bike or how to swim. Becoming a stepmother is a bit like all of these, and we too need the odd stabiliser or buoyancy aid at times!

There is one word that sums up the building blocks you need to establish (as well as the stumbling blocks you'll have to push to the side) and that is **PRACTISE**:

> **P**artnership
>
> **R**esentment
>
> **A**mbiguity
>
> **C**oping
>
> **T**ime
>
> **I**ntegration
>
> **S**upport
>
> **E**x-factor

Don't expect to run before you can walk and don't have unrealistic expectations of an idyllic family life from day 1. You will get there in time with determination – and practice.

PARTNERSHIP

The relationship you have with your partner is the most important relationship you can have in your stepfamily. It is only by keeping your relationship strong that you can be the best parent and step-parent you can be. It's vital to the success of your stepfamily. If you're content in your relationship with your partner you can work through any problem together. In Chapter 2, I'll help you to assess how strong your relationship is and discover if there are any areas you can improve on. There will be guidance on how to work together to resolve your problems, how to address the thorny issue of discipline (of the children that is – not your partner!) and how to set realistic expectations of each other. Above all, this chapter will help you to learn how to communicate effectively and make the most of any time you get together as a couple.

RESENTMENT

It's not unusual for stepmothers to start to feel resentful and angry about their situation. Often they feel as though they have no control over a situation that ultimately affects them but because they have no official 'status' as a parent, they can't step in. Many others resent the changes in their lifestyle, perhaps taking on more responsibilities in the household or feeling that their efforts aren't appreciated. The feelings can lead to resentment or even anger. In Chapter 7, I'll help you identify any resentment you might feel and understand the causes of your resentment or anger as well as giving you practical help in reducing these negative feelings, which should in turn improve your relationship with both your partner and stepchildren.

AMBIGUITY

Role ambiguity is one of the biggest problems for step-mothers. Women find it really difficult to define their role in the family. Are they a parent? Are they an 'extra' mum? Are they a friend? Should they be responsible for setting the rules and disciplining the children? Should they attend parents' evening or the Christmas school play? There are no rules for stepmums or stepfamilies and most find it takes time to work out what role they have. The trouble is working it out can be stressful! I discuss the issues of role confusion or role ambiguity in Chapter 7, and help you clarify your role in the family, with advice on setting boundaries and realistic expectations.

COPING

Different types of people cope with stressful situations differently; however, some coping mechanisms have been shown to work better and more effectively, and some coping styles – such as burying your head in the sand or avoidance coping – are unlikely to solve anything in the long term. Chapter 5 will guide you through the various ways of coping that have been shown to be more effective and more likely to lead to a successful outcome for everyone involved.

TIME

Most people underestimate how long it can take to develop relationships within a stepfamily. As is probably true for all relationships, the first two years are generally understood to be the most difficult, as both adults are trying to work out the new rules. Obviously, some things are easier to negotiate and compromise on than others but generally over time we find a way of working in harmony with our other half. Unfortunately, stepfamilies are likely to have more complex problems to deal with, with stepchildren and ex-partners to complicate the negotiations. So it's not a surprise to discover that stepfamilies take longer to develop than first families. By following the advice given in Chapter 4, you can reduce the time it takes you to get to where you want to be.

INTEGRATION

Some stepfamilies find it hard to bring together the two 'biological halves' of previous families and continue to divide their stepfamily along biological lines. Some stepmothers will urge their partner to spend time with their children without them, believing that they need the time together. While this is absolutely fine for some of the time, it's important that the children see you as a family unit, doing things together with everyone involved. Stepfamilies who rarely do things together often find it much harder to develop strong relationships between each other. I discuss the importance of including everyone within the stepfamily in Chapter 4, and show you how you can build a more integrated family unit.

SUPPORT

Everyone needs support from those they love, whether it's from their partner, friends or family. Lots of research has shown that if we don't get the support we need then our emotional health suffers and we're more likely to suffer from depression or anxiety. And the more support we get, the happier we tend to feel! In Chapter 6, I'll discuss the specific difficulties in stepfamilies that stepmothers are likely to face and show how we can all learn to get the support we need, when we need it.

EX-FACTOR

Many stepmums find that they struggle with the constant presence of their stepchildren's biological mother in their lives. Whether it's phone calls to the children, time with their partner or favouritism with the in-laws, the ex-factor is a major thorn in many women's lives. So it's important to learn how to control the impact they have on your lives. Chapter 8 will help you understand why you resent the role the ex has in your family and to identify the different types of ex. Is your partner's ex simply jealous or maybe overanxious – or perhaps just lonely? By understanding why they're reacting the way they are, you can change your behaviour to cope more effectively.

No one said it would be easy, but being a stepmother can be very rewarding, particularly if you can benefit from the experience of others. So good luck and happy reading. I hope you can use this book to work through any difficulties you may have in your stepfamily and learn to become a happier stepmum.

1

You as a Stepmother

Unlike first families, which begin with two adults, step-families are formed from two disparate family units, with children at different stages of their lives. You might inherit stepchildren as babies, teenagers or adults with their own families. They're all different but each brings with them their own challenges. Your stepchildren may live with you all the time or live with their mother most of the time and just visit for weekends or holidays. You might already have children of your own that you bring into the new stepfamily and you and your partner may go on to have children together.

First families all start from the same position. No children. Stepfamilies are formed with ready-made children. As a new mum you automatically get to be a member of a club called parenthood, bringing you together with other mums in the same position. You can share problems and worries and slowly gain confidence as a mother. As a stepmother you've joined a very different club but one whose membership is altogether more confusing! Not only is it difficult to find other stepmums to talk to, often you find that their position is very different from your own. For example, your stepchildren may be very small, while theirs are teenagers; or maybe your stepchildren live with you all the time while theirs just come to stay at weekends. Although you can share some of the frustrations of the role, it's likely that you're stressed by different issues. In my experience, it can be very hard to find friends that truly understand the unique challenges that the role can bring – or be able to offer useful advice.

So before we go any further, let's take a moment to identify some key differences *between* stepmums. As I've just said, it can be frustrating trying to find other stepmums who are in the same position as you, but while stepfamilies vary in many ways (such as the ages of the stepchildren or how many children there are in the family), there are fundamental family characteristics that can affect the way you approach step-parenting and the type of difficulties you're more likely to face. These revolve around whether your stepchildren generally reside with you and your partner or visit for weekends and holidays; and whether or not you already have children of your own from a previous relationship.

While some issues are common for all stepmothers there are generally distinct differences between stepmothers based on where the stepchildren predominantly live and whether the stepmother is also a biological mother. I like to refer to this as your 'step type'. Once you understand your step type you'll find it easier to deal with the specific issues you're likely to face within your family.

WHAT TYPE OF STEPMUM ARE YOU?

Take a moment to study the two statements opposite and decide whether you agree or disagree with them. Your answers to these will define your step type.

Statement 1:
My stepchildren live with my partner and me for the majority of the time.
Agree / Disagree

Statement 2:
I have biological children from a previous relationship.
Agree / Disagree

If you agreed with both statements 1 and 2 above then you are Step Type A. Your stepchildren live with you pretty much full-time and you also have children of your own.

If you agreed with statement 1 and disagreed with statement 2 then you are Step Type B. Your stepchildren live with you and your partner for the majority of the time but you don't have children of your own from any previous relationships.

If you disagreed with statement 1 and agreed with statement 2 then you are Step Type C. Your stepchildren live for the majority of the time apart from you and your partner, usually with their mother, but visit regularly. However, you also have children from a previous relationship.

If you disagreed with both statements 1 and 2 above then you are Step Type D. Your stepchildren come to visit your home regularly but live for the majority of the time somewhere else. You don't have any children from a previous relationship.

STEP TYPE A

If your stepchildren live with you and your partner for the majority of the time and you also have children of your own from a previous relationship then you belong in this category. As it's still predominantly the mother who cares for children following the breakup of a relationship (in about 80 per cent of cases), fewer stepmothers fit into this category. Cassie's story is typical of a stepmother in this position.

Cassie met her partner Phil six years ago. She had been a single mum for two years and had a three-year-old son. Her partner lived with his two daughters, now in their teens, after his first wife had died three years previously. Cassie's relationship with Phil soon became serious and after dating for a year they decided to move in together. Cassie really loves Phil and the girls but is constantly exhausted trying to keep the house clean and tidy, wash everyone's clothes, cook for a family of five every night and work part-time. Although she doesn't regret moving in with Phil and the girls she hadn't quite bargained for the extra work that seems to go with the job! She gets on really well with the girls though. They know she's not trying to replace their mum but they do enjoy being able to talk to her about things that their dad isn't quite so good with. Cassie would like to find a way of feeling less tired all the time. She also feels guilty that she doesn't spend as much time with her son as she would like as she always seems to be rushing everywhere. She would just like a break every now and again but that isn't very likely.

This type of stepmum often finds it easier to truly feel part of the stepfamily as they take on a much more traditional mothering role to their stepchildren. These stepmothers have a great deal of parenting responsibility. In addition to their own children, they are caring for their stepchildren full-time, which means they have increased physical, emotional and financial demands that go with it. Because of these extra demands they have to take care not to let the pressure get to them and avoid sinking into depression. The biggest problem this type of stepmother typically faces is in maintaining a balancing act between the demands on their time, finances and love.

Women who find themselves in this position often feel so snowed under with the pressures of looking after their partner, their children and their stepchildren that they rarely have time for themselves. It's important to make that time – whether it's coffee with friends or a night at the pictures with your partner. With all the children around all the time it's vital that you get a break from the stresses and strains of family life. If your stepchildren are old enough, rope them in to help. If you work full-time as well, see if you can afford to buy in some help with the housework – or bribe the children! If you find it hard to get time out because the children are younger, call on friends or neighbours to help with babysitting. If possible, you could even set up a babysitting circle where you can trade favours with your friends. Time, finances, love – work out which you're struggling with most and talk to your partner to try and find ways to help. Often it's the small things that make the most difference.

Cassie solved the problem of feeling tired and emotionally drained by sharing some of the chores around. She told Phil that she was feeling exhausted all the time. The house was much bigger than she was used to and seemed to constantly need cleaning or tidying. Phil and Cassie sat the girls down and explained that they needed to start doing their bit in the house, beginning with their bedrooms. They also agreed that one night every week the girls would cook dinner (with a bit of guidance!) so that Cassie got a night off. Cassie had been so busy dealing with the day-to-day trivia that she and Phil never got the time to talk properly. By making time for each other they were able to understand what was really important to each of them.

STEP TYPE B

If your stepchildren live with you and your partner for the majority of the time but you have no children of your own from a previous relationship then you belong in this category. As with the previous category it's still quite unusual to be a stepmother in this position, but it still includes up to one in five stepmothers. As you'd expect, this type of stepmother tends to feel part of the new family relatively quickly as they are together as a family unit for the majority of the time. However, Type B stepmums sometimes suffer from greater feelings of resentment towards their role and often believe that they have less support from family and friends. Many women become stepmothers at relatively young ages. The stark contrast between single girl and wife and stepmother can come as quite a shock to the system! As their stepchildren live with them all the time, women in this position can feel that they have no time to develop their relationship with just their partner. Others struggle with the emotional difficulties of bringing up their stepchildren when they desperately want a child of their own. Sometimes, these plans have to be effectively 'put on hold' until they can afford to have another child. As Fay told me:

> I feel very frustrated. I look after my stepchildren, Molly and Tom, because I love my husband, Dave. When their mum wasn't able to cope of course we stepped in. But my life is so different now. I gave up my job to look after them so I don't see much of my friends any more. For a long time I really struggled as I'd had no real experience with children. Barely any of my friends had partners, let alone children, so I felt I had nothing in common with anyone any more. All the other mums at school seemed to know each other and I felt really left out. It's got better over the last year but it was a really lonely time. It's not their fault but I really resent them being with us all the time. We never seem to get a break.
>
> FAY, STEPMUM FOR THREE YEARS WITH TWO STEPCHILDREN AGED FIVE AND THREE

The contrast between Fay's single life and her new family life could not be more extreme. Fay clearly feels she's been thrown in at the deep end and is really struggling to cope with her new-found responsibilities. When I spoke with Fay I suggested that she might want to consider going back to work part-time so that she sees more of her friends and feels less isolated. The children were also old enough to consider sending them to nursery so that Fay had time to recharge her batteries and regain a sense of independence. I also suggested that the grandparents might be delighted to give the couple a break by taking the children for the odd weekend.

It's really important to recognise that this type of stepmother is expected to make the greatest change to her lifestyle. If you find yourself in a similar position, make sure you catch up regularly with your old friends. Get as much support as you can from grandparents or other relations. It's all too easy to get dragged down with the stresses of family life and not make time for anything else. Don't bottle up your feelings. If you're frustrated then talk to your partner – or a friend, if you find it easier. But above all, avoid letting resentment build up and don't be afraid to accept all the help on offer – and to ask for it too.

STEP TYPE C

If your stepchildren live for the majority of time with their mother or another carer and you also have children of your own from a previous relationship then this is the category you belong to. Jane is typical of this type of stepmother.

Jane has lived with her husband Ian for two years. Her two daughters (aged ten and seven) from her previous marriage live with them full-time but also spend some weekends with their father. Ian also has a one-year-old daughter from a previous relationship. She lives with her mother for the majority of time but comes to stay with Ian and Jane for weekends and the odd day during the week.

Ian and Jane are really happy. They manage to get plenty of time together when her children are visiting their dad and Ian's daughter is with her mum. But Jane finds herself struggling with feelings of jealousy and resentment when her stepdaughter comes to stay. Ian is great with her daughters but when she sees the way he looks at his daughter she can't help feeling sad and a little jealous that he doesn't feel the same way towards her children. She knows that it's unreasonable to think he would but she can't help her feelings. Jane finds that she almost dreads the days when her stepdaughter visits. Their routine has to change to fit in with the toddler. And while Ian spends time with his daughter she concentrates more on her girls so they don't feel left out. Consequently, their weekends are becoming more separate, with Jane spending time with her daughters, and Ian spending time with his. Jane is desperate to change things. She really loves Ian but is struggling with her feelings towards her stepdaughter.

Jane's feelings are common for women who find themselves in this type of role. As these stepmothers already have children of their own, the move to the new family is not such a big change and they tend to cope better with the transition, often with more confidence and less anxiety about how to deal with their stepchildren. However, they often find it more difficult to bond with their stepchildren than the fulltime stepmothers. Stepmothers in this position can find it hard to balance the demands of their stepchildren and their biological children. They worry that by showing affection to their stepchildren, their own children will feel left out. And as they only see their stepchildren for part of the time it takes much longer for them to develop a close relationship with them. The main challenge to this type of stepmother is including everyone within the stepfamily unit. As the stepchildren move in and out of the family unit for weekends, holidays or odd nights during the week, this type of stepfamily needs to adopt a flexible approach to parenting. And for the family to be successful and thrive, it's vital that the stepchildren are treated as an integral part of the family.

I suggested to Jane that she needed to modify her view of who was included in her definition of her family and accept that her stepdaughter is as integral to the family unit as her own daughters. The fact that her stepdaughter isn't there all the time doesn't mean she is any less of a member of the family; she just has a different schedule. I told her that whenever she finds herself feeling down and resenting her stepdaughter's visit she needs to focus on the positive things associated with the visit, rather than the negative: how much her husband has been looking forward to seeing his daughter, for instance; how much her stepdaughter must miss her dad during the week and how lovely it is for her to see him; how kind and helpful Ian is to her and her daughters. Sometimes when we expect a difficult time, such as during a visit from our stepchildren, that's what we look for, and this then reinforces our opinion that things are bad whenever they visit. Unfortunately, while we're looking for the issues we close our eyes to anything positive and miss the chances to build closer bonds with our stepchildren. If you see this happening in your family think carefully about the way you approach your stepchildren's visits. Even a small change in your mindset can make a huge leap forward in making visits more enjoyable and rewarding for everyone.

STEP TYPE D

If your stepchildren live for the majority of the time with their mother (or someone other than your partner) and you don't have children of your own from a previous relationship then you belong in this category. Over 50 per cent of stepmothers typically fall into this group. Women in these stepfamilies often find it difficult to fit into their new family and don't really feel they are part of the family unit. They can feel resentful of their stepchildren for the impact they've had on their lives. They are often confused about their role, which can in turn lead to them feeling anxious about their responsibilities. Some women try really hard to build a relationship with their stepchildren but if their efforts aren't appreciated they can be left feeling rejected and withdraw from their stepchildren to avoid further rejection.

Like Type C stepmums, these women look after their stepchildren for only part of the time. This makes it difficult for them to include their stepchildren in their definition of their family, particularly when they don't have any children of their own. They see themselves as a couple rather than a family and therefore often don't view the children as an integral part of the family unit. Consequently, some women find that they resent the times when their stepchildren visit. As Debbie said:

It's so much harder than I imagined. When I first met my husband I thought, I've got nine nephews and nieces who I love so that'll be fab, but all of a sudden, every other weekend we have to have his children and have to do things to entertain his children…I've got a hate like I've never experienced in my life. I'd never do anything to hurt them but I resent them.

DEBBIE, STEPMUM FOR FOUR YEARS TO TWO
STEPCHILDREN AGED 12 AND 9

Clearly not all women in this category suffer from these difficulties but the fact that many women are expected to take on parental responsibilities for their stepchildren without having any experience with children can lead to greater anxiety about whether they are doing the right things.

If you find yourself in this situation and are struggling to cope you must find time to sit down and talk to your partner. Make sure you both have realistic expectations. Your stepchildren are going to be a part of your life together but you aren't going to become an 'instant parent' to them. You both need to take things slowly. Learn to *like* your stepchildren and get to know them better. Find something that you can enjoy together, whether it's watching a film, baking a cake or walking the dog. Try not to feel apprehensive or negative about your contact time. While I would encourage you to spend time with them when they visit you don't have to be joined at the hip. Be clear with your partner that you want to help him look after his children and want to be part of the fun but you also need time out. In this way you are less likely to feel as resentful of their visits. If you find that you start to feel anxious when your stepchildren are visiting try and understand why. Are you confused about your role? Do you worry about when to get involved or when to stand back? Are you concerned about whether you're doing the 'right' thing? Do you worry about when to step in to tell them off or let their father take control? Lots of stepmothers in this position become anxious about these issues, which are all related in some way to defining your role in the family and having the confidence to be a stepmum. You need to agree with your partner on any changes that you think would help. Some things are non-negotiable – such as the visits themselves – but there are always things you can do that help you cope better. Learn to understand not *how* you feel but *why* you feel that way.

Here's an example of a conversation I had with Liz, a stepmum of two years to two stepchildren aged seven and nine, about the way she felt.

LIZ: I feel really resentful that the children come to stay every other weekend.

ME: Why?

LIZ: Because we have to entertain them all the time.

ME: Who says you have to entertain them?

LIZ: Well, if we don't they get bored.

ME: Have you tried letting them play on their own when they come?

LIZ: Well, no. We've always just organised lots to do. I end up resenting spending all weekend doing these things for them, which costs such a lot and they never seem to be grateful.

ME: So is it the money or the time that you worry about?

LIZ: Well, it's a bit of both I suppose. But what really annoys me is that they never say thank you to me.

ME: Have you mentioned this to your partner?

LIZ: No, I just sort of seethe about it and think how rude and ungrateful they are.

ME: Maybe you could talk to your partner and agree to encourage the children to appreciate the things you do but how about trying a weekend where you plan less but perhaps let them play in the garden or in a park? That way they learn to realise that they can't have activities planned all the time but also they learn to appreciate the times when you do make more of an effort.

LIZ: I guess we could try.

ME: Would that help you feel less resentful?

LIZ: It might. But I think my partner wants them to have a really good time when they come.

ME: Have you spoken to him about this?

LIZ: Well no, I just know he looks forward to their visits. But I guess I could talk to him.

When Liz spoke to her partner he realised that he was trying too hard to please his children. He felt guilty that he didn't see them during the week and wanted to make the most of their time together. But he agreed to try and take things easier and see how it went. The change seemed to go well for everyone. As the weeks went by, the children no longer expected to be taken out the entire time and just enjoyed playing or relaxing with their dad. Liz found that she was less resentful of the weekends and although she made sure she spent some time with them, she also found time to meet up with friends over a coffee or for a spot of retail therapy. She was grateful that her partner had listened to her worries and this made her more determined to make the weekends happy for everyone.

If you find yourself feeling resentful of your stepchildren in the way Liz did try and work out the true causes of your anxiety and put into place a plan of action. Sometimes if we're feeling anxious and confused, it can be hard to pinpoint the actual problem. Once you understand the cause of your anxiety you can start to deal with the problem, ideally with the help of your partner. So if, for example, you're frustrated because your partner's children don't seem to respect you and rarely do as they're told, work out a strategy with your partner. Be specific about their behaviour, such as 'Can we encourage the children to say "please" and "thank you" more often when they're with us' so that your partner understands the issue and can help you make a start on improving their behaviour. Statements such as 'your children are just awful and haven't been brought up with any manners' is simply going make your partner feel defensive about his children, rather than supportive of you. Don't expect any instant fixes though. As always, take things slowly and learn to recognise and appreciate any positive changes, however small.

COMMON ISSUES

As we've seen, there are broadly four types of stepmothers, based on the complexity of the family and where the children normally reside. But within each of these groups there are vast differences within the families. Some will have very young children or much older children; some will have children spanning a broad range of ages; others will have new children born into the new stepfamily. Some will find all the children get on like a house on fire – others will fight just like real siblings. As in first families, stepfamilies are all unique, just as individuals have their own personalities. However, the broad stepmother types that I've defined allow me to share with you the main strengths and difficulties that are associated with each kind of stepmother. By understanding these I hope I can show you how you can learn to cope with these challenges to join the growing numbers of happy and contented stepmums out there.

2

Your Relationship with
Your Partner

When couples decide to put their relationship on a more permanent footing – whether moving in together or getting married – they usually devote plenty of time to talking about the practicalities. Where will they live? Where will their children reside? Or, how often will they come to visit? Will the children share rooms or can they each have their own? Holiday as a family or separately? There's a whole host of things to consider as a new stepfamily which take time to discuss and agree.

But this is only part of the story. While it's exciting to plan and organise your new life together, it's extremely difficult to understand the emotional impact the changes may have on you and your relationship. You can plan for your stepchildren coming to stay for the weekend, you can decorate their room and you can cook them their favourite meal – but you can't plan for feeling like an outsider or confused about your role when they're around, or ensure you'll know how to interact with them. Unfortunately, there is no easy way to prepare emotionally for becoming a stepmother but the first step is to understand that any of these feelings – and others – are perfectly common and normal, but if you don't address them they can be incredibly destructive to your relationship with your partner.

None of these problems will simply go away on their own. If you don't deal with them they will just stack up and eventually become a series of mountains to climb. While you can't always predict the flashpoints in your relationships you must learn to recognise them and deal with them, one at a time. Inevitably you need to make sure you talk to your partner – and keep talking, until the problem starts to get smaller and is no doubt replaced by another – that is, until they're all gone and you find yourself concentrating on issues that *all* families have to deal with such as bad grades, untidy rooms, falling out with their friends, stroppy teenagers and so on.

MAKING YOUR RELATIONSHIP WORK

The media would often have us believe that people find it harder to stay together in remarriages or partnerships than first marriages. We're bombarded with statistics telling us that second marriages are more likely to fail and that remarriages are somehow less stable than first marriages. But the truth is that there is no real evidence to support this view. People are generally as happy in their remarriages as couples in first marriages – some research has even found couples in remarriages were *happier* together than those in first marriages, particularly in the early years of their relationship.

However, it is generally acknowledged that the presence of children from previous relationships can increase the stress within the new family, putting more pressure on the couple and their relationship. Experts think that stepchildren make it more difficult for the couple to find enough time together in the critical early stages of their relationship. It's in the early months and years where you learn most about your partner – their likes and dislikes, what makes them happy, how to drag them out of a bad mood, or the date of their mother's birthday. Without this special time together, couples miss out on the opportunity to get to know their partner and strengthen their relationship, making it harder for them to withstand the pressures of everyday life.

So as long as you concentrate on building your relationship with your partner in the early days, research suggests that your relationship is as likely as any other couple's – with or without stepchildren – to survive. The most important thing is to give yourself a solid foundation on which you can build your stepfamily. If you're happy with your partner and with your relationship you are likely to find it easier to adapt to your new role in the stepfamily. In other words: find ways of strengthening your relationship with your partner and everything else should slot into place that much easier. That's not to say it will all be plain sailing, but if you can find a solid base on which to build your new family you're more likely to survive the inevitable wobbles along the way.

SO HOW HAPPY ARE YOU WITH YOUR PARTNER?

Before I move on to talk about strategies for dealing with stress between yourself and your partner I'd like to take a few minutes to understand how much support you get from your partner and how happy you are with your relationship.

Please take a moment to respond to the following four statements as honestly as you can and add up your total at the end using the scores provided.

Statement 1:
My partner and I work together to resolve problems.

Strongly disagree	*1*
Disagree	*2*
Neither agree nor disagree	*3*
Agree	*4*
Strongly agree	*5*

Statement 2:
My partner and I have similar views on rules and discipline.

Strongly disagree	*1*
Disagree	*2*
Neither agree nor disagree	*3*
Agree	*4*
Strongly agree	*5*

Statement 3:
I find it hard to raise problems about my stepchildren with my partner.

Strongly disagree	*5*
Disagree	*4*
Neither agree nor disagree	*3*
Agree	*2*
Strongly agree	*1*

Statement 4:

I am very happy with my relationship with my partner.

Strongly disagree	*1*
Disagree	*2*
Neither agree nor disagree	*3*
Agree	*4*
Strongly agree	*5*

Now add up each of the four scores. You should have a maximum score of 20 and a minimum score of 4.

Score

4–9   Your relationship with your partner clearly needs a bit of work. Recognising this is the first step in making improvements! Use this chapter to identify the areas that you need some help with.

10–14   You and your partner don't always work as a team. Try and identify from your answers where the main issues are – or maybe you already know. Take the time to work out with your partner how you could make those important changes and improve your relationship.

15–20   A score of over 15 suggests that you have a strong relationship with your partner and are able to talk to them openly about any issues. It's important not to become complacent though! Make sure you keep talking and working together to resolve any problems.

WORKING TOGETHER TO RESOLVE PROBLEMS

It sounds so easy: just talk to your partner about your concerns – 'a problem shared is a problem halved'. Why is it then that we find it so difficult to talk about some problems, particularly when the problems are related to our relationship with our partner or our partner's children? Often stepmums feel awkward in talking about problems with their partner for fear that they will make things worse. So they soldier on trying to make the best of it. Sometimes we feel that our partners will somehow intuitively know what the problem is and miraculously fix it. But of course they're not mind readers. They may sense a problem but have no idea what the cause could be. If we bottle up our feelings they can start to overwhelm us – and the problem rarely goes away on its own. The best course of action is to talk about the issue with your partner. One stepmother, Susan, explained how this approach had recently worked for her:

> *My stepson visits us every other weekend but as his mum travels with work he often comes to stay with us while she's away. My husband, John, would arrange these dates with his ex-wife, but would forget to tell me. It wasn't that I minded my stepson coming, it was feeling left out of the planning that bothered me. No one seemed to consult me at all. It was as if I didn't count or matter. I didn't want to make a fuss as I didn't want John to think I wanted him to stop seeing his son. I just wanted to be kept in the loop.*
>
> *I'd had a really busy week and was really looking*

forward to spending a day with John – just the two of us. Instead I woke to find him getting ready to go to watch Joe play football who was then coming back to stay with us for the weekend. My reaction was completely out of proportion but I just broke down in tears. Poor John had no idea why! It was just the culmination of months of not quite knowing what was happening and when. I explained to John how I'd been feeling and he promised to make it work. We now have a family calendar with a column for everyone – including Joe. John makes sure that he puts all Joe's visits on here and tries to remember to tell me when there's a change. If Joe's mum is going away for a long trip, John makes sure he checks with me first so that there aren't any clashes. The changes weren't difficult but they have made a big difference to the way I feel.

SUSAN, STEPMUM FOR NINE YEARS
TO STEPSON AGED 11

Susan told me that although she was delighted with the outcome she was frustrated with herself for not speaking out sooner. Now that she's included in the family plans she feels so much more relaxed and not taken for granted.

If something is worrying you, or you find yourself getting frustrated or resentful, think about how you can raise the issue with your partner. Problems rarely go away on their own, they just tend to grow, leading to ever more frustration. It's a vicious circle that you need to break early on in your relationship. Don't expect your partner to know how you feel about something unless you tell him! If on the other hand you find that you do raise issues but you find it hard to resolve problems together then try to prioritise. If you are struggling with a particular problem, work out what the issue is for you and what you would like to happen. And be prepared to compromise. Find a time to talk to your partner when you're both calm and relaxed. Explain to him why you're worried and give him time to understand and ask you more questions. Talk to him about possible solutions, or things that would help you. It's not very helpful to simply raise problems without offering any possible solutions. Remember though, everything is a balance. Any solution has to be fair on everyone – not just you. Try and take things slowly and only fix one thing at a time! Learn what works for you both and appreciate small steps. As long as the steps are taking you in the right direction that has to be a good thing.

RULES AND DISCIPLINE

One of the other real bugbears in stepfamilies is the issue of disciplining the children. Step-parents have to tread a fine line, particularly in the early stages of a relationship, to impose the household rules without completely alienating their stepchildren. This thorny issue is discussed in more detail later in the book but it's worth raising it here too, as it can cause real issues between yourself and your partner if you don't agree on how you're going to impose household rules and who is responsible for disciplining the children.

Stepmothers are in a difficult position. On the one hand, they have a right to impose their own household rules just as any mother would. It's not unreasonable after all to expect older children to help with household tasks such as washing up or tidying their rooms or setting the table – particularly when the same rules apply to other children in the household. However, if you're constantly asking them to do chores it can feel like nagging and can lead to resentment from the stepchildren, especially if the rules are different when they are with their other biological parent. While this hostility can develop between you and your stepchildren, possibly more damaging can be the resentment that can build up between you and your partner if you feel they don't support you. Some stepmothers avoid setting rules and disciplining their children as they want to avoid being labelled a 'wicked stepmother', so often portrayed in fairy stories. So they stand back and expect their partner to impose the rules that they believe are reasonable and fair. If this doesn't happen they begin to feel resentful, not just towards their stepchildren but also towards their spouse.

So the important thing to remember about setting household rules and discipline is to make sure you agree with your partner about the roles you both take and share your views honestly with each other. It's only natural that you will have different views – most couples do – but you need to talk to each other about what's important to you and make sure that you back each other up to enforce any rules or discipline.

Communication

If you feel that setting and enforcing household rules and disciplining your stepchildren is causing conflict in your relationship with your partner take a few minutes to talk it through with him, calmly and rationally. As always, there are no right or wrong answers. Firstly you need to understand what your partner's view on this subject is and whether or not it's the same as yours. For example if your partner thinks that only the biological parent should be responsible for discipline and you think it should be a shared responsibility you need to find a compromise. It may be that you can agree that your partner will be responsible for the majority of the discipline issues but they will defer to you and support you when you feel you need to talk to your stepchildren about something. Alternatively, if you feel unsure about disciplining your stepchildren but your partner wants you to take more responsibility perhaps you could agree to take things slowly, with the proviso that he fully supports you in all your decisions. The key is to **agree** what works for **your** family and be **consistent** in your treatment of all the children.

When I spoke to stepmothers, there was a consensus among those that had been in their roles for some time. As Becky said:

> I think my stepchildren have two different worlds, each with different rules. You have to be really clear with them what the rules are in your household – even if

that's different from their other home. Paul and I would say, well you may not have to do this with your mum but these are the rules here. It did feel like Groundhog Day for ages. Every time they came to stay it was like starting over again from scratch. It took them a while to get used to the way we did everything but over time things have really improved. Initially I let Paul take the lead but I've got more confidence now and am much happier setting the household rules.

BECKY, STEPMUM FOR SEVEN YEARS TO TWO
STEPCHILDREN AGED 12 AND 8

You may find at first that you're unsure how to set the rules and deal with discipline issues but look to your partner for guidance until you find the confidence to be more involved in the decision- and rule-making process. Many stepmums find this approach works well, particularly those who don't have any children of their own. By taking things slowly and talking to your partner about what's important for you, you're more likely to get things right in the longer term.

BE BRAVE – TALK THINGS THROUGH WITH YOUR PARTNER

Many women feel uncomfortable about sharing their feelings about their relationship with their stepchildren with their partners for fear of hurting them. One stepmother had tried talking to her partner about her feelings early on in their relationship but later regretted it, believing that she had been too open and that resulted in a rift between them. She had since been more reserved in sharing her feelings, which had left her feeling isolated and frustrated. Another stepmother, Maggie, felt that although she was happy to talk to me about life as a stepmother she would be less open in her answers to me if her partner was with her. As she explained:

> He can be very sensitive about the children and he's very defensive so I have to be careful not to upset him. I feel like I'm walking on eggshells all the time. Even though the children can be naughty sometimes it's hard for me to criticise them as he always steps in and finds excuses for them. I just end up feeling really frustrated.
>
> MAGGIE, STEPMUM FOR THREE YEARS TO TWO STEPCHILDREN AGED SEVEN AND FIVE

So is this behaviour 'normal' or are these women simply storing up problems for a later date?

COMMUNICATION

Communication in stepfamilies is typically different than that in first families, with couples actually using less so-called 'negative communication', which involves criticism, anger and conflict. Instead, couples in a stepfamily often withdraw from conversation to avoid discussing difficult issues. While the fact that the couples engage in less-destructive communication is good, this leaves them more prone to unresolved issues within the family unit, which may in turn lead to more frustration and resentment. Not surprisingly, positive communication, which involves praise and recognition, is more likely to lead to happier stepfamilies than either negative communication or avoidance.

Many women find it difficult to broach certain issues with their partner, usually because they want to avoid hurting their partner or simply can't see a way out of the situation. However, women who have been stepmothers for several years often find that while they have found it hard to raise issues with their partners in the early years, over time they realise that it was more important to discuss things than let them fester.

> I think we've just got better at doing it, at talking, at me being brave enough to say things. You know in the early days he'd say things like, it's easier when all the children are here and now I'll say, do you know, it's not, it's a damn sight harder!
>
> MELISSA, STEPMUM FOR SIX YEARS TO FOUR STEPCHILDREN AGED FROM 16 TO 9

Clearly talking to your partner more to resolve problems has got to be a good thing. As well as reducing the conflicts in the family by improving the communication, you're likely to suffer less anxiety, leading to less stress and an altogether happier outlook – which is after all what we're striving for.

Constructive communication

If you find yourself struggling to understand your role in the family, or feel isolated, or simply find it difficult to deal with your stepchildren, how do you go about broaching these subjects with your partner without making things worse? The key is constructive communication.

Accept your feelings

As stepfamilies have complex relationships and complex problems it's natural that at times you will struggle with your feelings. Rather than trying to change the way you feel, understand why you feel the way you do and accept your feelings. You aren't to blame for the way you feel; however, you are responsible for the actions you take. Take some time to think about why you feel the way you do, why you feel angry or anxious or frustrated and try and understand how your partner might feel and work together to change over time.

Take responsibility for your own feelings

Don't fall into the trap of blaming your partner or your stepchildren. For example, saying 'You exclude me from the arrangements you make with your ex' is very different from 'I feel excluded when you make arrangements with your ex about the weekend'. In the first sentence you've placed the blame entirely on your partner. Your partner may not have meant to do this at all and is likely to disagree with you or become defensive. So rather than talk about how to change things, you can both become stuck in an argument which isn't going to achieve any-thing, other than make you both feel worse!

Confront the problem

The next thing is to confront the problem rather than deflect your frustrations at others. Instead of just shouting at your partner, explain what your anger is really directed at. Try and put aside some time to talk about the problem. Then try to agree a way forward together.

Focus on the problem

Always focus on the problem in hand. Don't get distracted by bringing in other more minor problems in an effort to bolster your case. Work out what the main issue is you want to address, and keep focused.

Remain calm

Once someone starts shouting to make their point the other person is rarely listening to what they're saying. It becomes a battle of wills, with no winner and no solution. Both parties just end up feeling angry and frustrated and less willing to start again!

While these tips are good for times when you need to talk to your partner about problems, remember that communication is not just about fixing things. It's about recognising good things, noticing when people make an effort or try and change their behaviour. By keeping a balanced outlook, you and your partner are more likely to have a realistic view of your relationship.

MAKE THE MOST OF COUPLE TIME

One of the main differences between first families and stepfamilies is the absence of time as a couple. Stepfamilies miss out on the initial years when it's just them and they have time to get to know each other, their likes and dislikes, and to build precious memories that they can draw on when times are hard. Remember that you're together as a family because you and your partner love each other and want to be together. Couple relationships in stepfamilies often suffer because they're established at a time when the adults have more responsibilities, both with their children and possibly their career. By contrast, first families tend to form when adults are younger and have fewer ties, allowing them to devote more time and attention to their partner. It's important to create those times for couples in stepfamilies to keep their own relationship strong and able to withstand the pressures of everyday life.

Make sure that you find time to be together – just the two of you. Make regular dates – once a week, once a month or every third Tuesday! It's not really important how often you can find the time. What is important is that you prioritise your relationship and make sure you keep the dates. Find a babysitter or friend to look after the children or better still, if your children and stepchildren spend time with their other biological parent, use the time they're with their other family as 'your time'. This kills two birds with one stone – not only do you get time alone with your other half but if you also have children, you'll find that you have less time to miss them or dwell on what they're up to while they're visiting their father. Instead of counting the hours until they get back you'll find that the time just flies by. Enjoy time together as a couple and talk about what you want for your family and about what's important to you. Pamper each other, cook a nice meal together, go to the cinema or just go for a romantic walk. It doesn't matter what you do or how much it costs – as long as it's something you can enjoy together. You could also use the time alone to discuss things that are worrying you or upsetting you, with the knowledge that you won't be interrupted. In that way you can be refreshed and ready to deal with the onslaught when the children come back.

IMPROVING YOUR 'QUALITY OF LIFE'

So hopefully I've shown you (or maybe just reminded you!), how important it is to spend some quality time with your other half. But you may be saying, 'Well that's all well and good for those stepmothers who have a break and only look after their stepchildren for some of the time. What about us full-time stepmums? How do we get time off?'

Obviously, it's easier to find time alone with your partner if all the children in your stepfamily spend time with other biological parents at some point. If you look after your stepchildren, and possibly your own children as well, full-time, it can be trickier to find time together. But you must persevere. Given the busy lives you lead, juggling the various children, running a home and possibly working as well, you are more susceptible than most to the stresses of stepfamily life, which can affect not only how happy you are but how well you cope.

In recent years, health professionals have started to look at something called 'quality of life' to try and understand the types of issues people face. Quality of life generally covers a broad range of areas including each person's physical health, such as whether they need regular medication and whether they suffer from any pain; their psychological well-being, measuring how content or down they generally feel; their social relationships, such as whether they have a partner and whether they have a good network of family and friends to rely on; and finally their environment, which includes their finances and their living arrangements. By understanding an individual's quality of life, experts hope to be able to identify areas to help people more effectively. Research on the quality of life of stepmothers suggests that full-time stepmothers have a much lower overall quality of life compared to part-time stepmothers or biological mums.

These findings reflect the extra pressures that full-time stepmothers face and highlight how important it is for them to make more of an effort to find time away from their children and stepchildren to strengthen their relationship with their partner. There are also differences between the various types of full-time stepmothers. Type B stepmothers, for example, often find it more difficult than Type A stepmothers to maintain their social lives when they become part of a stepfamily. Some stepmothers I spoke to said that they felt isolated from their friends who didn't understand their new responsibilities. The stepmothers found the stark change from being a single girl about town to a full-time mother difficult to cope with and while they happily threw themselves into their new roles many felt this was at the expense of their social lives. Quality of life is also a good indicator of an individual's overall well-being such as their levels of depression and anxiety, with low quality of life linked to higher depression and anxiety. So it's even more important to look at ways of increasing your quality of life to avoid spiralling into more negative feelings and eventually depression.

Whatever type of stepmother you are, it's important to find time apart from the children and, as a rule of thumb, the harder it is for you to organise the more important it's likely to be for your happiness and well-being. So start now. Make that date and get planning!

THE BIOLOGICAL DAD'S STORY

Although many women find the transition to the role of stepmum hard to navigate, it's important not to forget the role of their partner. They have to jointly deal with the problems but they may see things from a very different perspective. As one dad said:

> I knew things weren't easy for Sally. We moved in together three years ago. She hadn't got any children but I had a son aged three from my previous marriage. Sam came to visit every other weekend and while I couldn't wait for his visits I began to realise that Sally was much less enthusiastic. She would start to become moody before he came and this started to lead to rows between us. Although she didn't say anything I thought that she just didn't like Sam. Looking back,

I guess I was frightened to talk to her because I just didn't know how I was going to fix the problem. So I sort of buried my head and ignored it for a long while. Eventually though, things came to a head before one of Sam's visits. She broke down and told me that she just didn't know what to do when he came. As she didn't have children she didn't know how to cope and felt really anxious when he came to stay. She also felt left out of any plans. I realised that I had been making things worse because I was trying to keep Sam 'out of the way', as I thought she just didn't get on with him. We spent a lot of time talking and over time things really improved. I realised that I hadn't really thought about how Sally felt. I was so wrapped up in seeing Sam that I forgot how hard it must be for her. We now spend time together as a family at least one day over the weekend and the two of them now get on really well. Although making the first move was hard, I'm so glad we started talking.

JOHN, DAD TO SAM AGED SIX

As John's story illustrates, it's all too easy to think you know what the problem is but unless you start talking to your partner you're in danger of getting it very wrong. While I've talked about how stepmums can improve their relationship with their partners through constructive communication and setting realistic expectations, it's important to look at things from the father's perspective as well. Here are just a few of the things dads can do to help create a happier stepfamily with their partner.

Tips for the biological dad

➤ Don't expect your partner to be a 'replacement mum' to your children. You can expect her to be supportive but be careful not to heap too much responsibility on her too soon.

➤ You all need time to adjust to the changes but especially your partner and your stepchildren. They need time to get to know one another and to learn to trust and respect each other. Your role is to help build their relationship together.

➤ Keep communication lines open. Make sure you make it easy for your partner to talk to you about their worries. Becoming defensive about your children will only discourage your partner from raising issues in the first place.

➤ Jointly agree with your partner on the rules and discipline you want in your family and make sure you always support your partner, particularly in front of the children. You must present a 'united front', otherwise your partner is likely to feel confused and resentful.

➤ Make sure you tell your partner about any plans you have with your children, such as when they're coming to stay or any changes to the routine. It's important that your partner feels included in all family decisions.

Remember *every* family – whether they are first families or stepfamilies – has problems to deal with. The trick is to work with your partner to resolve them. Don't expect your partner to read your mind and just 'know' what's worrying you. Talk to them, calmly and rationally and without attributing blame. Take time to set realistic expectations for the way your new family is going to work and agree on them. And most importantly, make time for you and your partner and you're on your way to becoming a happier stepfamily and a happier stepmum.

3

Understanding Your Relationship with Your Stepchildren

I would say that I'm really close to my stepson, I mean I've known him since he was two so he's sort of grown up with me around. So we do get on well together but although I love him, it's not the same feeling that I have for my own children. It's just a different kind of affection. I wish I did feel the same but I just don't. Last week, for example, we were all getting ready to go out when my stepson threw a tantrum. It wasn't over anything important – I think he wanted to go to the park with a friend and we said he couldn't. He got really angry and just said he didn't know why he came to visit us anyway. I remember feeling really irritated and thinking well, don't bother then if you don't want to. Then I thought about it and realised that I would have reacted so differently with my children. Yes, I'd have told them off for being naughty but I'd have wanted to make up and cuddle them afterwards. I felt really guilty but I guess I just have a different emotional bond with them.

KIM, STEPMUM FOR SIX YEARS TO EIGHT-YEAR-OLD
STEPSON, MUM TO DAUGHTERS AGED FIVE AND THREE

Kim had been a stepmum for over six years. Although she was happy in her stepfamily and, as she said herself, felt she had a good relationship with her stepson, she realised that there was a difference in the love she felt for him compared with her love for her children. This is a perfectly normal reaction and one shared by almost all stepmothers. There are many common stepfamily myths but one of the most common is that you will automatically and instantly love your step-children just because you love their father. They'll feel the same about you and you'll all live happily ever after. Sadly that's not the reality. You may have met and fallen in love with your partner but that doesn't mean that the same thing will happen when you meet his children or he meets yours. It will inevitably take time to develop your relationship together. You need to get to know your stepchildren, grow to like them and nurture your relationship over time.

Think about the times you've met other people's children. Although some are angelic, others are simply monsters! How often have you breathed a sigh of relief when your friend finally leaves with her unruly children in tow or you thank your lucky stars that you only have to look after your son's friend until teatime and not a moment longer! Children are all different, just like adults, and while we love the company of some, others are just harder work. So why should it be any different with our stepchildren? Some relationships work better than others because of our person-alities. We can be drawn to certain people because we see traits in them that we admire or value. If we don't feel we have as much in common with individuals we find it harder to get closer to them and to build a bond.

SET REALISTIC EXPECTATIONS

One of the main challenges stepmothers face is in setting realistic expectations about their new family with their partners. When asked in one study whether they had changed their expectations during the time they had been in their relationships, over 80 per cent of stepmothers felt they had lowered their expectations. Many said that as a result of this they had learned to step back or become more detached and to expect less closeness or love from their stepchildren. These stepmothers also felt that their husbands had similar unrealistic expectations of the stepmother role, with many expecting their partner to be more like a mother to their children and to be more involved with them. Researchers have found that those who believe that stepfamily life should mirror a traditional nuclear family in this way are far more likely to encounter difficulties in their relationships than those with more realistic expectations. So let's be specific about what I mean by 'realistic' expectations. I've listed some of the more common ones below – it's not a definitive list but should give you a flavour of what I mean by unrealistic!

Unrealistic vs realistic expectations

Unrealistic Expectation	Realistic Expectation
I'll have 'nice' stepchildren who will be well behaved all the time.	My partner's children will be normal kids with good and bad points just like everyone else. That's just part of their personalities and I have to accept that.

Unrealistic Expectation	Realistic Expectation
The more I put into my relationship with my stepchildren the more they give back.	I shouldn't do anything for my stepchildren expecting anything in return – they're children! I should do things because I want to and because it's the best thing for all the family.
I'll be their new mum.	I can't ever replace their mum but can be an 'extra' adult that can learn to love and support them over time.
Our new family will replace their old one.	A stepfamily is a new type of family. It can't replace the old one but can be just as good or even better – just different.
My stepchildren and I are bound to love each other immediately – because I love their dad.	I want to get to know my stepchildren so that we can learn to like each other and hope that love will grow over time.
My relationship is with my partner – it has nothing to do with my partner's stepchildren.	My relationship with my partner has to include his children – they're part of his life too and we need to work together to build a new family unit.

The main thing you should take from this is the need to think more about what you expect from your relationship with your partner and your stepchildren. If you expect too much too soon, you're likely to be disappointed – lower your expectations and remember to focus on the positives rather than the negatives. Use this as a starting point to build on and you might surprise yourself at how much easier the job gets over time! But above all, give yourself time to adjust and adapt to your new family.

MANAGING YOUR EXPECTATIONS

It's important that you and your partner agree on your role in the stepfamily as any confusion can lead to more tensions in your relationship. Equally it's vital that you both have realistic expectations about your roles and the development of your family.

Take some time to look again through the list of realistic and slightly more unrealistic expectations given above. Ask yourself whether you are being realistic in your outlook or whether you're being a little too optimistic. Or maybe it's your partner who needs a small dose of realism? Maybe he expects you to look after the children and the household in the same way as his ex-partner did? If necessary, reset your expectations: better to start with lower expectations that you can build on over time. Okay, your stepchildren won't automatically love you on day 1, but why should you expect them to? They need to get to know you before they can begin to enjoy being with you. Love comes a long way down the line. And why strive to be a 'normal' family – whatever that is? A stepfamily is just a different type of family – perfectly 'normal' but maybe a little more complicated!

Consider the following question and think about how you might finish off the sentence below. How do you see your role? Remember there is no right and wrong; it very much depends on your family circumstances, such as whether your stepchildren's mother is still a part of their lives, how old the children are, whether the children live with you all the time or just some of the time and how long you have known them. The most important thing is that you agree with your partner – that your expectations are matched.

I think a stepmother's role is to be…

> ➤ a 'replacement' mother
> ➤ an 'extra' parent to help and guide the children
> ➤ a friend not a parent
> ➤ just there to support their partner

Once you have decided what you think your role is, talk to your partner and check that they have the same expectations. If your partner's views are different from yours, take time to listen, to understand why they think the way they do. Similarly, make sure your partner understands what your expectations are and why. Try and compromise.

Most stepmums, when asked what they think their role is in the stepfamily, find it much easier to say what the role *isn't* than what it *is* – suggesting that they find it tricky to actually define their role!

I think the problem is that there are no role models for stepmothers: you know what a mother and father are supposed to do but not a stepmother. It's not a mum but it is a parent. I think step-parents can be just as close (as parents) and three parents are better than two.

KATE, STEPMUM FOR FOUR YEARS TO HER SEVEN-YEAR-OLD STEPDAUGHTER

I don't consider myself a stepmother, I just see myself as someone who is married to someone who has a child from a previous relationship. I'm her dad's wife and there's a difference. The word 'mother' conjures up a nurturing aspect which is not something I associate with my stepdaughter.

FIONA, STEPMUM FOR 12 YEARS TO 15-YEAR-OLD STEPDAUGHTER

I really don't know what my role is. My husband's son and his partner have just had a baby daughter, but as I wasn't around when my 'stepson' was growing up I don't really feel that I'm related to the baby. They have all the 'grandparents' to turn to for support and I sort of feel surplus to requirements.

SHEILA, STEPGRANDMA FOR 20 YEARS TO ADULT STEPSON AND BABY GRANDDAUGHTER

All these examples illustrate the difficulty in defining your role as a stepmum – or even a stepgrandmother. There aren't any fixed rules to guide you, it's really up to you and the rest of your family to work together on understanding the best role that you can play in your stepfamily. Sheila, for example, felt terribly isolated in her family. While she desperately wanted to be considered a 'grandma' to her husband's new granddaughter she didn't know how to broach the subject with her family. She reasoned that as the grandchild already had a 'full set' of four grandparents there wasn't room for her. I asked Sheila why there was a limit on four grandparents and why her granddaughter couldn't have a fifth? After speaking with Sheila I realised that no one had told her she couldn't be a grandparent, it was just one of the rules she'd established herself. Once she understood that the only real barrier to her becoming a grandparent was herself, she felt more confident about being able to change the situation and take a more active role with her new granddaughter.

The difference in the perception of the role and expectations, however, may also be affected by the type of stepmother you are. Full-time stepmothers, for example, spend the majority of time with their stepchildren and as such play a larger role in their stepchildren's lives. It is therefore more reasonable to expect this type of stepmother to feel that they are fulfilling a parenting or mothering role. On the other hand, part-time stepmothers only care for their stepchildren for the minority of the time and may feel more comfortable assuming a more supportive role to their partner. Additionally, the complexity of the stepfamily also plays a part in defining role expectations. Women who already have biological children may find it easier to adopt a closer parenting style to their stepchildren. However, women who don't have any prior parenting experience may be more comfortable, particularly in the early stages of their relationship, to take a back seat and work on building trust with their stepchildren rather than trying to parent them too early. This 'friendship style' approach to step-parenting can be more effective than trying to be an extra parent to their step-children, particularly in the early stages of their relationship. In this way the relationship between the step-parent and stepchildren develops slowly, allowing each of them a chance to get to know the other.

Remember, the key is to manage your expectations. If your partner is expecting you to step into the mothering role and you want to be a friend to your stepchildren, or vice versa, the chances are one or both of you will be frustrated and disappointed, not to mention the confusion that this would cause to your stepchildren.

MEETING YOUR STEPCHILDREN

The first time your partner introduces you to his children is likely to be a daunting experience. For those of us who have already gone through this we'll remember all too well feeling anxious and apprehensive about meeting them. What will his children be like? What will I say to them? Will they like me? What sort of things can we do together? We all want to make a good impression on our partner's children but at the same time it's uncharted territory. And don't forget to spare a thought for the children. Depending on their ages, they're also probably going to feel a little daunted at the prospect of meeting Dad's new partner. You may be the first partner – other than their mother – that they've seen their father with. They're bound to worry about how the change is going to affect them and their relationship with their father.

The secret to making sure things go as well as possible is in the preparation. It's only when your relationship has become serious that you need to consider meeting and starting to get to know your partner's children. How much your partner tells his children about you depends on their age and maturity. Young children simply need to know that Dad has a special friend that he'd like them to get to know, whereas older children will recognise that Dad is seeing a girlfriend and will want her to meet them once the relationship becomes more serious.

Make sure that your partner tells his children something about you before they meet you so that they know what to expect, and try and find out things about them too. What activities do they like doing? Are they interested in a particular sport? Is there a subject they like at school? What's their favourite food? Knowing something about their lives will keep the conversation going when you meet them and show them that you've taken an interest in them. Try and build your relationship with them slowly. It will take time for them to feel comfortable with you – and vice versa. Let your partner take the lead and be happy to fit in with their plans. It's also a good idea in the early stages to let your partner still spend time with his children without you so that the children don't feel things are changing too quickly. One of the main reasons children are wary of their parents' new partners is the worry that they will interfere with their own relationships with their parents. They need reassurance that your involvement is not going to affect the time they get to spend with their father.

Tips for preparing to meet your stepchildren

➤ Encourage your partner to talk to his children about you – before they get to meet you.

➤ Make sure the information is appropriate to the age of the children. Young children want to know simple things about their dad's friend, such as what they look like and what they're called; older children will understand the significance of the relationship and should be trusted with more details such as how long you've been dating and how serious the relationship is.

➤ Take an interest in their lives. Know their favourite sports, foods or activities.

➤ Take things slowly. Don't expect to be their best friend after a few meetings. Building a relationship with them will take time and effort.

➤ Assure them you aren't trying to replace the other parent. You're an extra person to talk to, play with and ultimately care for them.

WHEN YOUR PARTNER DOESN'T SEEM TO WANT TO INTRODUCE YOU TO HIS CHILDREN

As I've said, meeting your partner's children is not something to rush into. You and your partner need to be sure that you have a strong relationship that you are both committed to before you meet his children or he meets yours. But what if you feel your partner is dragging his heels? What if you've been together for some time and you still haven't met his children? Maddie has been seeing her partner for over a year but has yet to meet his 12-year-old daughter.

David and I have been going out for about 15 months now but he keeps his life with his daughter totally separate from his life with me. I think we have a really good relationship and we've even started to talk about possibly moving in together later in the year but I'm worried that I still haven't met his daughter. His relationship with his daughter's mum broke up seven years ago and his daughter lives with her, but David sees his daughter every week and I think they've got a really close relationship. But I just feel like he's not letting me into that part of his life and I'm worried about making any more commitment to him.

When I spoke to Maddie, she told me that as far as she knew, David hadn't introduced any of his previous girlfriends to his daughter either. Clearly he was struggling with combining his two worlds – his girlfriend and his daughter. Because Maddie hadn't met David's daughter she admitted that she generally put her to the back of her mind and rarely asked him about her – not because she didn't care but because she didn't feel included in this part of his life. By doing this, though, Maddie was maintaining the status quo and not pushing for change. I encouraged Maddie to break this cycle and start to talk to David more about his daughter, to get to know her likes and dislikes and her personality. She asked David if he would start to tell his daughter about her, so that his daughter could begin to accept that her father had a partner. Over the next few weeks Maddie and David talked more openly about his daughter and David admitted that he had been worried about taking the next step in his relationship with Maddie. He was worried how his daughter would react and didn't want to jeopardise their close relationship. However, he realised that if they were to move on in their relationship it was important that Maddie met his daughter.

If you still haven't met your partner's children and feel the time's right, start to talk to your partner about your concerns.

1. Explain to your partner that you want to get to know his children – they're an important part of him and will affect your ongoing relationship.
2. Listen to his concerns. Perhaps things have gone wrong in the past, maybe his ex has become jealous. Make sure you understand the reasons behind his views.
3. Agree a way forward. It may be that he wants to wait a bit longer. Accept that, but agree to discuss it again after a set time.
4. Keep talking to your partner about his children. After he's spent time with them, ask him what they did together, whether they had a good time and what they enjoyed doing. It may feel hard at first but it will help you get to know more about them before you meet.
5. Don't resent the time your partner spends with his children. Remind yourself that this makes him a caring, responsible father – qualities that probably attracted you to him in the first place.
6. Be patient. Meeting your partner's children for the first time is a big step in any relationship. Don't try and rush into things before your partner's ready.

MOVING ON IN THE RELATIONSHIP

When you start to get to know your partner's children it's natural that there will be a certain wariness between you for some time. After all, you don't know each other very well, you have no history together or shared memories. You're starting from scratch. Often in this situation it's hard to think of anyone else's perspective other than your own. You're all going through major changes and it's hard enough to cope with your own feelings let alone think of anyone else. But the reality is, your stepchildren are probably finding everything very difficult to take on board and understand what you being on the scene is going to mean to them. Jess was six when her dad moved in with his new partner. Jess had met Caroline a few times before she moved in with her dad but they hadn't spent much time alone and Jess didn't feel she knew her very well.

I didn't really know what to expect when Dad moved in with Caroline three years ago. I lived with my mum for most of the time but went to visit Dad and Caroline every other weekend. She seemed really nice at first but she was really different from Mum. She got really stressed about things that Mum didn't seem to mind. I had to remember to tidy my room all the time and help clear the dinner table. I didn't mind helping but I just kept forgetting – which made her and Dad cross. Things are much better now though. We get on really well and I enjoy seeing her with Dad. I was worried in the beginning that I wouldn't get any time with Dad but

things didn't really change. Dad just seems happier.
Everything is very different in their house from my home
with Mum but I don't mind now I've got used to it.

JESS, AGED NINE

As Jess said, it was hard for her to adjust initially to the new rules. She just wasn't sure what to expect or how things would change for her. But once they all got used to living as a new family everything became much easier. While you may feel it's difficult to know what your role is in the family, it's equally difficult for your stepchildren to know how their relationship with their father might change now that you're part of the family unit. First of all they need to accept the change. It may be that they have got used to seeing their father on their own and now feel they somehow have to share him with you. If you also have children, your stepchildren need to get to know them as well and somehow learn to get along together. They may still have been hoping that their parents would get back together some time and obviously your being there is not going to help that happen! But whatever their initial reactions, they have to accept the change before they or you can move on with building a relationship.

Once there is a general acceptance it's time to start building a bridge of trust between you. It's very hard when someone you don't know asks you to 'trust them' as you have no basis on which to assess the risk. Are they likely to let you down? How do you know? Your stepchildren need to learn that they can trust you and rely on you. And often actions are far stronger than words. I was talking to Alice, a teenager who was worried about her dad's new partner.

Alice is aged 15 and lives for the majority of the time with her mum and younger brother. Alice and her brother visit their dad and stepmum every other weekend. She used to see her dad more often but since he's moved house he's further away from Alice's home and can now only see her at weekends. Alice told me that she really tried to get on with her stepmum but has now given up as she feels her stepmum doesn't want her around. They used to go out together – shopping, just the two of them, when her dad had first introduced them to each other. Alice really enjoyed getting to know her stepmum but that seems to have stopped now. When they first met, her stepmum tried to reassure Alice that she wouldn't take her father away from her. Now Alice feels that's exactly what she has done. Since her dad moved in with her stepmum Alice has seen much less of him and things seem really awkward when Alice and her brother visit. Her dad always has to check things with his partner before he can agree anything with Alice. Her stepmum rarely spends any time with her and Alice feels she resents her coming to stay. Her dad and stepmum always seem to be arguing and Alice senses it's probably to do with her as they always go quiet when she walks in the room.

Sometimes it's hard to put yourself in someone else's shoes. Is Alice being given a hard time or should we feel sorry for the new stepmum? The arguments that Alice senses may have nothing to do with her. But how do they resolve their problems if no one is talking to each other?

When I spoke to Alice's father and his partner it was clear that they didn't know how to resolve the mess. Alice's father hadn't noticed that there was a problem, while Alice's stepmum was finding it hard to cope. Things were hard financially since moving house and that was causing more arguments between herself and her partner. She had tried to get to know Alice but didn't think Alice really liked her and so had decided to let her partner spend time alone with his children when they visited. She admitted that she did feel pangs of jealousy when Alice came to stay but was ashamed that she felt this way. She wanted Alice and her brother to enjoy their visits but just didn't know how to improve things. So Alice and her stepmum were both struggling with the situation while Alice's father was doing a perfect imitation of an ostrich. Once he was persuaded to raise his head from the sand he could start helping build the bridges between his daughter and partner.

This story illustrates the danger of just taking one perspective on a problem. Both Alice and her stepmum were unhappy but neither of them was talking to the other – or anyone else – about their difficulties. To start resolving the problem, Alice's dad spent time with her explaining to her the reasons for the move. Although he hadn't wanted to move away from his children he couldn't afford to live any closer. He told Alice how much he looked forward to their time together and reassured her that she wasn't the cause of any arguments. He just didn't want to involve her in his problems. They made sure that they spent time together as a stepfamily, but Alice asked if she could go on the odd shopping trip with her stepmum. Her dad made her realise that she hadn't really told her stepmum how much she'd enjoyed their time together. Now Alice makes sure that she shows her appreciation to her stepmum when she spends time with her and lets her know how much she has enjoyed being with her. Alice's stepmum now feels part of the family unit and enjoys time alone with Alice, getting to know her better. She feels much more secure and has managed to banish any feelings of jealousy. Spending time with her partner's daughter has made her realise how much Alice misses her dad and how important it is for them to spend time together.

Developing your relationship with your stepchildren

1. Give everyone plenty of time to adjust to the changes. Remember, if your stepchildren only visit every other weekend it's going to take longer to build relationships with them than if you see them more regularly – or if you live together all the time.

2. Don't expect to become their new best friend. Learn to recognise small changes in their behaviour to you like giving you a hug when they come to visit or asking your opinion of something rather than turning to their dad.

3. You can't expect instant love but you can, and should, expect them to show you respect. If that's not happening make sure your partner talks to them and makes them understand how you expect them to behave in your home.

4. Try and find something that you can do with your stepchildren on your own that can become a shared activity. With teenagers it may be going out shopping or planting

flower seeds with younger children. The activity itself doesn't matter: what's important is finding something that you can enjoy together and helps you get to know each other better.

5. Make time to do things together as a family, to create shared memories and experiences.

6. Don't feel that you have to be there all the time but try and balance your time so that if they're visiting you get to see them for some of the time.

7. If you're finding it hard to get on with your stepchildren, try and talk to your partner about your worries. Avoiding the issue won't make it go away and will only distance you from the family unit.

8. Be consistent with your stepchildren. Let them know the rules in your home so that they know what's expected of them.

9. Empathise. Don't be tempted to just think about how you're feeling: try and consider your partner and your stepchildren as well. It's hard for everyone to adapt to the new family unit.

10. Learn to recognise and enjoy the good times. Build happy memories to sustain you through any difficult times.

PUT YOURSELF IN YOUR STEPCHILDREN'S SHOES

The saying that you never know how someone's feeling until you've 'walked in their footsteps' is never more appropriate than describing stepfamily behaviour. As we've seen, it's all too easy to become absorbed in your own problems and not consider how others might be feeling.

If you're struggling to understand your stepchildren or have started to dread their visits or even make yourself scarce when they're around, take some time to think about how *they* might be feeling. It might help you understand why they're behaving the way they are. For example, your household may be very different from your stepchild's other home. While they spend the majority of time on their own with one parent they might find it hard to adjust to step- or half-siblings at your home. They can go from single child to one of many in the space of a car journey. Or it could be the opposite, and it takes them all weekend to calm down and enjoy the peace and quiet of your home. Perhaps your partner has been single for a long time and your stepchildren have to get used to sharing their dad. Take some time to think about the circumstances that brought you together as a family and how your stepchildren might be feeling. Use the checklist below to start things off.

➤ How long is it since your partner separated from your stepchildren's mother? If it was fairly recently the children may still be hoping for a reconciliation; however, if it was some time ago, your stepchildren may have got used to spending time with their dad on their own and resent you 'taking him away'.

➤ Do they have stepsiblings or half-siblings at your home or with their mother? Do the households have similar numbers of children or are they quite different?

➤ Do your stepchildren have space to call their own when they come to stay or do they have a spare room? Do they feel welcome and wanted?

➤ Are there things for them to do in the local area? Do they have friends to play with? Could they be lonely?

➤ What kind of responsibilities are they given in both homes? Are they treated the same?

➤ What are the ages of your stepchildren? Teenagers, for example, will want to spend time with friends at weekends and may resent too much time spent with family.

➤ How long have you been together as a family? If things are still new, expect to take things slowly.

Once you've spent some time putting yourself in your stepchildren's shoes, take the next step and work out ways that might improve things for them – and by default you. So, if for example your house is always full of children and you think your stepchild may be finding it hard to adjust to being only one of many, try and find them some space to call their own. Even if it's not possible to give them a room of their own, try and give them some personal space that they can call theirs. Make sure you give them some storage, maybe drawers or even a cupboard, where they can keep spare clothes or toys or anything else that they treasure and want to keep safe. Or perhaps your partner has been on his own for a long time before settling down with you and his children are finding it hard to share his attention. Make a point of letting them know that you know how important it is that they spend time together. If, on the other hand, there isn't anything you feel you can specifically change, it may be just a case of biding your time. Talk to your partner about your concerns and make sure he helps in trying to build your relationship with your stepchildren. It's important that he gives you the time and space to get to know each other. Stepfamily research has found that while stepmothers recognise that they have a weaker bond with their stepchildren than their own children, their bond with their stepchildren gradually does get stronger. Stepmothers often feel that their relationship moves from a purely functional role to a more emotional and involved role over time. Lily's dad married his new partner five years ago when she was just eight. She told me:

> At first I really didn't like the idea of having a step-mum. I was used to visiting my dad on his own and it felt weird having to share him. I don't think I was really very nice to her at first – she probably dreaded my visits! I hated it when she tried to tell me off as well. I didn't see why she should, but I remember Dad telling me that it was her home as well and I needed to listen to both of them. Over time I got used to her being there and started to enjoy seeing her as well as Dad. We get on so well now. It's really nice having someone to talk to that cares about you, but isn't your mum or your dad.
>
> LILY, AGED 13

DEALING WITH DIFFERENT RULES AND DIFFERENT VALUES

Let's state the obvious. Your stepchildren are not *your* children. They are your partner's children. So don't expect them to behave as if they're yours because you're setting yourself up to be disappointed. One of the major gripes from stepmothers

I've spoken to is that their stepchildren seem to have different values from them. Often they feel that their stepchildren are spoiled or have poor manners. As one stepmother said:

> *I really don't like my stepchildren, which is a horrible thing to say. In my opinion they are quite spoiled – they have everything at their mum's and everything at their dad's, but they just don't seem to appreciate anything. They are quite materialistic and that's not me...I would bring them up very differently if they were my children.*
>
> CATHY, STEPMUM FOR EIGHT YEARS TO TWO STEPCHILDREN AGED 12 AND 10

If you can empathise with this it's important not to place the blame solely on your stepchildren. Although you can't change your stepchildren's mother's behaviour, you can talk to your partner about your worries. Often, part-time dads feel guilty that they don't see enough of their children and try and make up for the lost time by buying gifts. Talk to your partner and try and make them realise that they don't have to do this. Their children just want to spend time with them. If they do expect presents it's probably just because that's what they've got used to!

Children are very adaptable and can usually cope well with having two homes and the different rules and regulations that go with that. It's up to you and your partner to set the ground rules for your household and it's not unreasonable to expect your stepchildren to stick to those rules – even if they are different from the ones they have in their other home. They'll soon learn what's expected of them as long as you're fair and consistent. So if one of your rules is that your stepchildren set and clear the dinner table, make sure you remind them and thank them each time so that they get used to the rules. The most important thing to remember is that every rule needs to be reinforced a number of times before it becomes second nature. So don't be disheartened if you have to keep reminding them – just make the house rules clear to everyone and make sure you're consistent. Remember though, if your stepchildren don't come to visit very often it can take them time to get used to the different house rules. Every visit can seem like groundhog day as you feel you're back to square one each time – but persevere and you will get there in the end.

While it's vital that you and your partner establish some clear ground rules in your household it's equally important that the rules aren't enforced at the expense of everything else. I recently spoke to a young boy, Tom, who was finding it difficult to accept his dad's partner.

I visit my dad and stepmum every other weekend. I look forward to seeing them but my stepmum seems to have a go at me the moment I arrive. Before I've even got in the front door she's shouting at me to take off my shoes – and when I'm playing with something, the moment I finish she's shouting at me to put it away and keep things neat and tidy. She just doesn't seem to trust me to do anything on my own. All the time I am there my dad's constantly reminding me to ask Belinda if I can help her with the housework.

I don't mind helping but I just don't seem to get a chance to relax and spend time with them just talking or playing.

TOM, AGED 12

Clearly, Tom's dad Andy and stepmum Belinda have some rules that they expect him to obey. The problem is, they're not giving him a chance to show that he understands the rules! I spoke to Andy and Belinda and encouraged them to put a bit more trust in him and try and be more relaxed. Belinda explained that as she didn't have any children of her own, she wasn't used to having children around and found it hard to cope with the changes that seemed to surround the visits. We agreed that perhaps she could step back a little and give Tom the opportunity to show that he did respect their rules. Over the next few visits things improved dramatically. Belinda realised that she had become really stressed before each visit and had become too focused on making sure Tom fitted in with their lifestyle.

If Belinda's behaviour and feelings strike a chord with you try and change your mindset. Don't expect or look for problems when your stepchildren visit – look for the positives instead. Yes, it's important that your stepchildren understand and follow your household rules but try and be supportive rather than dictatorial. Praise them when they do something good – thank them for remembering to take off their shoes, for making their bed or setting the table. This reinforces their behaviour and encourages them to do it again. Give them a gentle reminder if it looks like they've forgotten – but give them a chance to remember first!

LACK OF ACKNOWLEDGEMENT

It's very common for stepmothers to feel taken for granted. They look after their families day after day, week after week, with barely a 'thank you' from anyone. The daily grind of cooking, washing and cleaning is just expected to happen, with freshly laundered clothes miraculously appearing in wardrobes and bathrooms cleared of soggy towels and tide marks round the bath. But is this any different from non-stepfamily households up and down the country?

Ask any mum and they'll tell you a similar story. Children just expect things to happen for them – even the most well-mannered and well-behaved children. While they may be eternally grateful when you can turn round a particular item of clothing for that special event or be delighted to find you've cooked their favourite dinner, generally they fail to notice the fluffy towels in the bathroom or the fact that you've spent the day cleaning the house from top to bottom. But that's normal, isn't it? Children can't be expected to notice, or appreciate, these normal mundane things. And we shouldn't expect our stepchildren to be any different.

It's a bit of a conundrum. On the one hand we want our stepchildren to blend into our families seamlessly, but on the other we want them to show some appreciation for looking after them so well. I suppose it's not surprising that we're all confused about our roles from time to time!

So should we just learn to accept the lack of acknowledgement from our stepchildren? The short answer is most definitely no – but it's not that straightforward. If you have your own children as well as stepchildren this is slightly easier because the answer is that you should expect your stepchildren to behave in the same way as your children. It's up to you to set the rules. If, for example, you expect your children to say 'thank you' after a meal then you should expect the same thing from your stepchildren. The same goes for anything else you do for them. Be fair and treat all the children the same. You shouldn't expect your stepchildren to behave differently because that would mean they didn't think of your home as *their* home, even if it is only for part of the time. Try and turn the argument around. If they are relaxed and take things for granted the chances are they are comfortable in your home and you've helped make them feel that way.

However, if you don't have children of your own but just have stepchildren it's harder to make a comparison. You can't compare your children to nephews or nieces or even friends' children as they don't live with you. Your home is your stepchildren's home – whether that's all the time or part of the time. It's more than reasonable to expect your stepchildren to display good manners and be polite – but don't expect them to notice how much you do for them.

Here's how one stepmother dealt with this problem:

My partner has four children from his previous marriage. When we first moved in together I was shocked by the amount of work I was expected to do. I was trying to work and juggle the children. It was an endless trawl of shopping, cleaning, cooking and washing and with not a 'thank you' among them. After six months I was ready to throw in the towel and after a particularly hard day just exploded at my husband about the unfairness of it all. He was a little taken aback as he hadn't realised how unhappy I was. As we discussed everything it became apparent to me that if the children weren't going to show me their appreciation (and why should they) then my husband had to make up for it. Ever since he's shown me in small ways how much he appreciates me. It might be surprising me by cooking the evening meal one day, or taking me out for lunch or buying me my favourite flowers. It's made a real difference to my outlook. First of all it relied on me to change my expectations and secondly for my husband to recognise and appreciate my help.

NAOMI, STEPMUM FOR EIGHT YEARS TO
FOUR STEPCHILDREN, MUM TO TWO CHILDREN
AGED SIX AND FOUR

The message is, don't expect acknowledgement from your stepchildren – or any more than you would from your own children. But do remind your partner of the things you do for everyone and ask him to help restore some balance.

DIFFERENT AGES – DIFFERENT PROBLEMS?

It's difficult to generalise when talking about stepfamilies and stepchildren. You may have been reading this chapter thinking that the advice doesn't apply to you. Your stepchildren may be too young to follow your rules – or too old to care! The age of your stepchildren, of course, makes a difference to the dynamics in your family.

The age of children when entering the stepfamily can have a significant effect on the overall success of the family unit. It can also have an impact on the development of the step-parent–stepchild relationship and the potential for bonding. Younger stepchildren, particularly when they are less than nine years of age, find it easier to accept a step-parent as part of their family and similarly, step-parents also find it easier to accept and bond with younger stepchildren. While this is great news for those of you with little ones, it comes with a word of caution. Younger children in general are more demanding and can be hard work as many of us, I'm sure, can testify! So make sure you look after yourself and take time out when you need it. Celebrate the fact that the cards are stacked in your favour for building a good relationship with your stepchildren but don't overdo things. Take things slowly and make sure your partner does their fair share of the extra work in the household.

If your children are older than this, though, don't lose heart. Yes, inheriting teenage stepchildren is likely to be harder than inheriting the smaller variety – but forewarned is forearmed. Teenagers are entering a phase in their development where they're already becoming less reliant on their parents and looking to their peers for more social interaction. Teenage stepchildren are no different; the last thing they're looking for is yet another parent. What they do need, though – and probably would value much more – is an adult they can talk to who *isn't* their parent. Becoming part of a new stepfamily can be quite difficult for teenagers. If their parents' separation or divorce is still quite recent they may be struggling to accept the split – or even hoping for reconciliation. Their father's new relationship makes them face the reality that the changes are permanent and they may be reluctant to accept their new family structure. This is likely to make your life harder, particularly in the early days. But the same rules still hold. You need to work with your partner to lay down the ground rules and stick to them.

And before we move on, just a quick note on differences between boys and girls. Although there isn't much research in this area, there is some evidence to suggest that stepdaughters are more difficult than stepsons – but only slightly! Boys tend to be more straightforward than girls, while girls are more likely to store things up and dwell on them. Boys tend to let off steam instantly and move on. Try and learn to recognise the signs. If your stepdaughter is quiet or withdrawn try and get her to open up – either to you or your partner. Consider spending some time with her – just the two of you. Find something that she enjoys, perhaps a girly day shopping, a bike ride or a visit to the park. Somewhere you can both relax and have time to talk. If you can understand the problem you have some chance of fixing it. Leave it to fester and you can store up even bigger problems further down the line.

ADDING TO THE FAMILY – NEW BABIES

The decision on whether to take the plunge and bring a new baby into an already complicated stepfamily is one that gives many stepmothers sleepless nights. Often it's not a straightforward choice, with some families struggling to cope financially with another mouth to feed, usually with financial support for the children from previous relationships. Even if another child is possible financially, there is the worry of how a new baby will change the family dynamics. After all, this child will be different from the other children in the step-family as it will be living with both its biological parents for the entire time. Will that be difficult for the other children to cope with? Will you be able to treat this child the same as the others? Will it change your feelings to your stepchildren? These are the sort of questions which plague stepfamilies who consider adding children to their families. And, of course, the answer is not black and white. There are so many different things to consider, so many different permutations within families that no one can categorically tell you what the right answer is.

Pros and cons of adding to your family

Pros	Cons
A new baby is likely to bring a more integrated, connected stepfamily.	The stepmother may develop conflicting feelings between her biological and stepchildren.
A stronger bond between the stepmother and stepchildren is likely to develop.	The stepchildren may display feelings of fear, anger and jealousy towards the new baby, feeling it may somehow displace them in the family.
The new baby forms a kind of 'bridge' between the biological and stepfamily members.	The birth of the new baby may reduce the involvement of the stepmother with her stepchildren.

Pros	Cons
If the baby is the stepmother's first child she is likely to suffer less anxiety and ambiguity with her role.	A new baby inevitably brings increased stress as both parents struggle to adapt to the changes, putting more pressure on their relationship.

Despite early worries about the changes that a new baby might bring to their family, many stepmothers have told me how having a child with their partner improved their step-family in so many ways. The new baby seemed to bring everyone closer together and makes them feel part of the same family, with a kind of biological connection between all the members of the stepfamily – even though the stepmother isn't related directly to her stepchildren, her biological children with her partner are related to her stepchildren. Lots of research has shown that when a child is born into a stepfamily its members are more likely to include everyone in their definition of their family. The new baby has somehow blurred the lines between stepfamily and biological family. There's no longer a clear distinction.

It changed me in every way. It changed my perception. My stepchildren are now related to me, not just by marriage but by my baby.

STELLA, STEPMUM FOR FIVE YEARS TO TWO STEPCHILDREN AGED EIGHT AND SIX AND MOTHER TO BABY OLIVIA

I think it's made a difference for me having my own children in all sorts of ways. It almost completes the circle and there's a sort of bridge between my children and my stepchildren. I've got my own children and there's a connection between them and their half brothers and sisters.

Jo, STEPMUM FOR THREE YEARS TO TWO STEPCHILDREN
AND MOTHER TO TWIN GIRLS AGED ONE

Some stepmothers told me how they felt that they had developed a closer and stronger bond with their stepchildren since having a child. The changes were the starkest for stepmothers for whom this was their first child. Becoming a mother after being a stepmother seems to help women cope better, resulting in less confusion about their role in the family. They become less anxious in their relationship with their stepchildren and their confidence grows.

Overwhelmingly, the stepmothers I've spoken to about this felt that the birth of their children had a predominantly positive effect on their stepfamilies. However, they did find that they had to navigate through a few issues along the way. Although it rarely proves to be a problem some women worry that they will not be able to treat their children and stepchild in the same way. In particular, for women who didn't have their own children prior to forming the stepfamily, they worry that their feelings for their stepchildren will change and they will somehow be inferior to their feelings for their children. Eleanor had looked after her stepson full-time for the last six years with her partner. Although he saw his biological mother occasionally, Eleanor was to all intents and purposes his mother. They had a very close relationship and she loved him dearly as her own son. When she became pregnant her main worry was that she would treat her two children differently and that she would start to feel differently towards her stepson. Thankfully, none of her worries were justified. Her stepson absolutely adores his new brother even though he knows they don't share the same biological mother, and Eleanor loves them both equally.

However, while the experience of bringing a baby into a stepfamily for many women is a positive one, it should be recognised that it's a very personal decision and shouldn't be swayed by the impact it could have on existing relationships. The birth of any child brings with it enormous change in any family – step or otherwise – and needs careful consideration. While a baby is unlikely to make a happy stepfamily unhappy, it's almost certainly not going to make an unhappy stepfamily happy.

Some research has suggested that when stepmothers have children they become less involved with their stepchildren but it's likely that this is only temporary and is probably no different to all families when new babies arrive. A baby usually hits a family like a whirlwind. We all know that things are going to change but somehow you can never quite be prepared. Babies need lots of attention, particularly in the first few months, but as everyone settles into their new routine, life generally reverts to something approaching normality. Some parents try and lessen the shock of a new baby to their existing children. They build up the excitement, how they are expected to 'help' mummy with the new baby. Sometimes they're rewarded with a present 'from the baby' when it's finally born, with the parents hoping their children will accept the new family addition! However, some stepmothers have found that their stepchildren are less than happy at the prospect of a new half-brother or -sister. This can be in the form of jealousy or anger.

> *My 21-year-old stepson, as soon as he found out I was pregnant, yelled at his dad, saying that he had no right to have another child and it tore me apart. It was so hard in the first few months of my pregnancy knowing that there was someone in the house who didn't want the baby to be born.*
>
> SAM, STEPMUM FOR FIVE YEARS TO STEPSON AGED 21

Or it could be the fear that they're somehow being replaced, or checking their status in the family ranking.

> *When we took my stepson to visit my new baby for the first time he turned to his dad and said, who do you love the most, and my husband said, you'll always be my number one boy. I was really cross with my husband. I don't think he handled it very well at all. Obviously his son was worried that the new baby might take his place in some way, but he needed to know that his dad would still love him the same but would also love the new baby just as much. He needed to understand that it wasn't a competition.*
>
> NATALIE, STEPMUM FOR TWO YEARS TO STEPSON AGED FOUR AND MUM TO BABY SON

Some stepchildren are obviously going to worry about how the new addition is going to affect them – just as any child in any family might worry. It's important to think about how they might be affected by your decision to have a baby.

Your children should be the first to know that you are expecting, but don't expect them to be necessarily as enthusiastic as you are about the news. Even if they are excited make sure they know they can talk to you if they have any questions or worries.

How children react will depend on their age to some extent, whether they've already experienced a new baby in the house and on their existing relationship with each of you. If you have a good relationship with the children it's likely that they will adjust well to the changes, but you must try and reassure them that they will be just as important to you as ever, even though you may have less time together for a while. If your relationship with the children isn't particularly strong it's possible that they may see the new baby as more of a threat to them. They may worry about being left out or even replaced. If this is the case, you need to spend time with them, reassuring them that you love and care for them and that the new baby won't change that. Make sure you devote time for things *they* want to do, to reinforce that you care about them and want them to be happy.

While there are clearly emotional issues to deal with, try and minimise the practical changes a new baby will bring. For example, try and leave the children in their existing bedrooms so that they don't feel they're being displaced by the baby. If space is difficult and you do have to move them, make sure you involve them in any changes. Perhaps they can redecorate their new room or rearrange a shared room so that they keep their own space.

RELATIONSHIPS BETWEEN STEPSIBLINGS

Relationships between stepsiblings are very difficult to predict. They could get on like a house on fire or hate each other with a passion – or they may simply tolerate each other. There could be personality clashes, where the children simply don't get on with each other, or there could be jealousy between them – either emotional (you're getting attention from my father) or material (why do you get the biggest bedroom) or even different beliefs and values which make it difficult for them to develop any tentative relationship.

If you find that things aren't harmonious between the children in your family, try out the following:

➤ Find out what the main issue is, why the children dislike each other. Make time on your own to talk to your children to find out how they feel about your partner's children. Ask your partner to do the same with his children.
➤ Help them see the situation from the other child's perspective. For example, explain how it may be difficult for your stepchildren to feel part of the family if they only visit occasionally; or how they might find it hard to 'share' their dad's time.

➤ Talk to them about their feelings. Help them understand why they might feel the way they do. Try and reassure them that any worries they might have are unfounded.

➤ Tell them that although you understand their feelings, which may be jealousy, anger or even frustration, they still need to make an effort to get along.

➤ Look for compromises that make stepfamily life more peaceful for everyone. If, for example, your children resent having to share their bedroom when your stepchildren visit or have to move rooms, consider redecorating or rearranging the rooms to give everyone their own space. Make sure that all the children respect each other's possessions and ask before borrowing toys!

Above all, though, if the children don't get on in your stepfamily be patient and give them time to adjust. While you have made the decision to move in with your partner, your children haven't usually been part of those decisions. Hopefully you will have spoken to them about the prospect of moving in together and how they feel about the changes, but ultimately the decision is yours. They may need more time to come to terms with the changes and time to get to know each other. Once their initial worries start to fade they may start to find things in common with their stepsiblings and even begin to enjoy their company.

DIFFERENCE BETWEEN LIVE-IN AND VISITING STEPCHILDREN

Your relationships with your stepchildren are bound to be affected by how often you see them. If they live with you permanently there's more pressure on all of you to fix any problems you might have in your relationships – which is reflected in the fact that full-time stepmothers generally report better relationships with their stepchildren than part-time stepmothers. But if you only see your stepchildren once in a blue moon, the fact that you don't really get on is probably not something you lose sleep over. The majority of stepmothers, however, see their children every other weekend, which is quite a significant amount of time, especially if you don't see eye to eye with each other.

Type A stepmother families (see page 16) look after both their own children and their stepchildren all the time. As all the children live predominantly in the same home it's vital that they get along together. But as we've discussed, the simple fact that the family is together all the time helps the integration. As a stepmother in this type of family you have to make sure that you treat all the children the same and apply the same rules to everyone. If the children don't get on with each other you need to try and find some common ground between them. Although these children are stepsiblings they live together as brothers and sisters and are bound to have the usual quarrels and fallings out as all siblings do from time to time. Recognise that this is completely normal but identify any longer-term issues between the children. Above all, don't let resentment build. If there is an ongoing problem between the children make sure you and your partner act as intermediaries to help mediate and ultimately resolve the problem. Obviously, the family dynamics are also going to be affected by the ages of the children.

CHILDREN AND STEPCHILDREN BOTH FAIRLY YOUNG (PRIMARY SCHOOL OR YOUNGER) AND OF SIMILAR AGES

Apart from being rushed off your feet, your main challenge is to devote enough time to each of them. If you can, try and find a little time for each child individually, whether it's a bedtime story, help with homework or watching them play a sport. Make them feel special, each in their own way, to try and reduce any jealousy or resentment for the other children.

CHILDREN AND STEPCHILDREN SIMILAR AGES BUT MORE INDEPENDENT (SENIOR SCHOOL / TEENAGERS)

They will all still appreciate being made to feel special but perhaps in a less 'hands-on' way. Remember to ask about their friends or maybe the music they're into. Show that you're interested in what they're doing but recognise their growing independence.

CHILDREN AND STEPCHILDREN VERY DIFFERENT AGES AND HAVE LITTLE IN COMMON

It's important that you don't always rely on the older ones to be responsible for the younger ones. While it's fine occasionally, don't make it a habit, as the older children could easily start to feel resentful of the younger ones. And when you do ask for their support make sure you show your appreciation and don't just take it for granted.

Type B stepmothers (see page 18) look after their stepchildren for the majority of the time but don't have any children of their own from prior relationships. One of the main difficulties faced by this type of stepmother often lies in their lack of parenting experience. Although they don't have children of their own they are suddenly faced with being a stepmum to someone else's children. This can lead to real anxiety as they struggle to know how to parent their stepchildren, often with little or no feedback on whether they're on the right track.

If you find yourself in this position make sure you have the support you need from your partner. Take things slowly and build your relationship with your stepchildren over time. Recognise that while looking after your stepchildren full-time is difficult you can turn it into a positive. Most stepmums have to manage the fact that their stepchildren have two homes and two sets of rules. As your stepchildren live with you for the majority of the time, you and your partner have the most influence on them and they're less likely to be confused about household rules or have to cope with differences between their homes. Many stepmums in this category are also considering having children of their own (see page 80). The important thing to remember is to continue to treat all the children fairly and by the same rules. This is even more important when you have biological children and stepchildren who may be more sensitive to their differences. So although it's perfectly common and normal to worry about how you'll feel towards your stepchildren once your baby is born, the reality is that there is rarely a problem and the positive changes generally far outweigh the negative.

The main challenge for the **Type C** stepmum (see page 20) is in integrating the children into the stepfamily even though they spend only part of their lives with each other. While her stepchildren only live with them for part of the time, her own children often live with them for the majority of the time. The stepchildren have to manage the transition from one household to another, which may be very different environments. As a stepmother you need to understand how the children may be affected by these changes. Their position in the family can change, such as from being an only child to a middle child, or being the only boy to one of three; or their physical space may change, from having their own room to having to share with a stepsibling.

Stepchildren in this situation are more likely to feel envious or jealous of their stepsiblings. Why are they the ones who have to move between their homes? Why do they have to share their father with their stepsiblings? You will need to reassure your stepchildren that they are just as important as the other children. Try and make sure your stepchildren have a space to call their own. If they have to share a room, make sure they have their own bed and duvet cover, ideally one they've chosen themselves. Perhaps you could cook their favourite meal when they first come to stay and make sure that your children include them so they don't feel left out. Be clear about household rules and make sure all the children toe the line – they'll soon spot if someone is escaping duties and that could easily lead to open warfare! Be fair and be consistent – the watchwords of a stepmother!

Type D stepmothers (see page 23) have perhaps the starkest change to their families, moving from being a couple most of the time to an instant family when the stepchildren come to stay. Perhaps the hardest thing for stepmothers in this situation is dealing with their own emotions and learning to cope for the first time with living with children. Often the stepchildren come to stay at weekends, which may have been previously reserved for relaxing, going to the cinema or shopping. Suddenly, the house seems to be full of children who need to be looked after and entertained. The step-children may feel jealous of their stepmother. They may feel that she's somehow taken their father away, that they now have to 'share him' or fight for his attention. One stepmother told me that her stepchildren said to her that as she had their father all the time, it was their turn at weekends. Obviously, the stepmother didn't quite see it the same way. As they both worked full-time she barely saw her partner during the week and looked forward to their weekends together. The last thing she wanted was to spend the weekends on her own.

If you find yourself in this situation try and remember that your stepchildren miss their father and will look forward to spending time with him. Try and find a balance so that everyone gets something that they want out of the weekend. You could consider introducing a 'joker card' system. This is where everyone's allowed to play their 'joker' when they want to do something *they* like doing over the weekend. Make sure everyone gets treated fairly, so if you can't find time for everyone to do something they want over the weekend, they get first option next time you're together as a family. So, for example, if one of the children wants to go bowling, the whole family has to join in – even if it's not really 'their thing'. But once you've played your card you have to wait for your turn to come around again. Everyone gets a turn – including the adults – and there's no complaining. It's a good way to make sure no one feels excluded or left out from the family and could be used to plan weekends or even holidays. Perhaps if you find that you need to restore a little fairness you could implement something similar. It doesn't have to be expensive – put limits on the choices, but ensure everyone gets involved and has a bit of fun along the way.

I hope you now understand it's perfectly okay (and normal) to not have overwhelming feelings of love for your stepchildren when you first meet them. You need to give yourself and them time to get to know each other, your likes and dislikes, what you're good at – and perhaps not so good at. Build on small positive steps and learn to develop mutual trust and respect towards each other. It might help you to put yourself in their shoes, to try and see things from their perspective. You're not the only one having to face major changes in your life. They are too, and they have no control over the changes. This doesn't mean you can excuse any bad behaviour or rudeness but it might help you to understand the causes and help them come to terms with the new situation.

Try and spend time with each of your stepchildren on their own. Find something you both enjoy – not always easy, I know, but persevere. There are certainly some safe bets – teenage girls and shopping is one of those. Small children often enjoy baking or maybe even planting seeds in the garden; perhaps a trip to the cinema or bowling alley would appeal to older children. Once they like and respect you, they're more likely to listen to you and accept your way of doing things.

While we all want to be told how wonderful we are and what great wives and mothers we all are, the chances are no one tells us as often as we would like. Unfortunately, that's life. The chances are even slimmer that your children or stepchildren remember to tell you how great you are, how they enjoyed their packed lunch or how grateful they are that you washed and ironed their school uniform in time for school on Monday! We want our children to be polite and thoughtful but there are limits. Being a stepmother is not quite the same as being a mother. Sometimes we expect to be thanked for all the extra work we do – but we still don't get the thanks, and this can ultimately lead to resentment. Make sure your partner recognises your support and look to him for recognition – not your stepchildren.

And finally, for those of you thinking about having a child with your partner but are worried about the impact that might have on the rest of the family my advice is simple: don't rush into any decisions. Take things slowly and make sure that you're happy with your life as it stands. Ask yourself if your relationship with your partner is strong. Are you and your stepchildren comfortable with each other? Remember, it's unlikely that having a baby will make a previously happy stepfamily unhappy – but neither will it make an unhappy stepfamily happy.

4

Developing an Integrated Family Unit

One of the most common misconceptions that people have when they form a stepfamily is how quickly they think they will become a settled family unit. Relationships don't develop overnight and merging different expectations, different rules and different family traditions can take a long time. Everyone has to learn to adjust to this new environment and usually learn to make some compromises along the way. The integration of the new family unit can be impacted hugely by preconceived ideas about what should or shouldn't happen in a family. How many of you recognise 'oh, we don't do it like that at Mum's'? Each previous biological family will have had its own way of celebrating Christmas or birthdays or spending their time together at weekends or holidays. It will have had its own traditions and shared memories, built up over the years together. As a new family, everyone needs to learn to accommodate traditions from the past but also develop new ones that are unique to the new family unit.

It is a basic human need to have a sense of belonging to a group, and a family is a type of group that we all inherently belong to and identify with. When stepfamilies are first formed they bring together two separate groups that have little or no common ground between them. So long as these groups continue to identify themselves along biological lines rather than with the new stepfamily, the new family unit will struggle to develop.

The sooner individuals can begin to feel they belong to the stepfamily, the faster the family unit is likely to develop. The goal is to transform everyone's perception of the stepfamily from two separate groups to one inclusive family.

Who's in your family?

I'd like you to take a few minutes to truthfully think about your 'family' and write down all the members within it. The definition of family is entirely up to you – there is no right or wrong answer.

_____

_____

_____

_____

I've asked the same question to many stepmothers and got a whole range of answers – with some surprising results.

> From an emotional side I'd say my family was me, my husband and my baby but I think that it's naive and selfish of me to say that, because my family is myself and my husband, my stepchildren and my baby. If I had a choice I would just have my husband, my baby and myself but I don't have a choice.
>
> HARRIET, STEPMUM FOR FOUR YEARS TO TWO STEPCHILDREN AGED TEN AND EIGHT, AND MOTHER TO BABY SON

To be very, very honest, I would say it's me, my daughter and my mum and dad.

SUE, STEPMUM FOR EIGHT YEARS TO STEPDAUGHTER AGED 11 AND DAUGHTER AGED 10

My family consists of my husband, my children, my sister, my mum and dad.

VIVIEN, STEPMUM FOR SEVEN YEARS TO STEPSON AGED 13 AND MOTHER TO CHILDREN AGED FIVE AND THREE

My family is much closer since I had my baby son. There is myself and my husband, my son and my stepchildren.

ABIGAIL, STEPMUM FOR THREE YEARS TO STEPSONS AGED SEVEN AND FIVE AND MOTHER TO SON AGED ONE

So while some stepmothers don't include their stepchildren in their definition of family, others don't even include their partner, taking a purely biological approach to the word 'family'.

However, while it's difficult initially to bring together two halves of different families to form a stepfamily, it's important in the longer term to include everyone in your definition of your stepfamily, including those related by marriage or partnership.

If you're finding it hard to think of your new family in these terms use the tips in this chapter to help develop your own family characteristics and traditions. Hopefully over time, you will find a stronger sense of belonging to your new family.

The integration of a stepfamily can also be significantly affected by the types of stepfamily. If you are part of a residential stepfamily, where the stepchildren spend the majority of the time with you, you're more likely to find it easier to integrate everyone into the new family unit. As you're all together for most of the time it takes less time to establish the household rules, with little or no conflict from other households, and individuals have more opportunity to get to know one another and feel truly part of the same family unit. However, if you're a part-time stepfamily, where the stepchildren hop between families, it can be more difficult to include the children who are only with you for some of the time, particularly if you don't see them very often. There's also some evidence that the addition of a new baby to the family can increase the bonding between everyone in the stepfamily and improve the integration. But stepfamily integration is equally important to both types of family. As a part-time stepmum you'll need to work harder at creating a bonded family unit as you have less time during which you can develop your own rules, the special rituals and traditions that make your family unique.

DEVELOPING STRATEGIES

The onus for creating a unified stepfamily lies firmly with you and your partner. It's up to you to set the rules – both within your direct family and your wider circle of family and friends. You need to make it clear to everyone how your new family unit is going to function. So within the stepfamily it's things such as how you'll manage birthdays and holidays, and what you expect from each of the children in terms of helping with housework, mealtimes and discipline. Your wider circle of family and friends will need help in understanding how your new family is going to work.

Grandparents will need reassurance that they will still see as much of their grandchildren as before – but they might also have stepgrandchildren coming to visit. They will need time to adjust to these changes so make sure you give them this time. Don't be tempted to rush them into anything they're uncomfortable with. It may seem frustrating for you but it's far better to take things slowly and get it right than risk alienating the support from your family. Greg and his partner, Julie, realise now that by trying to force their parents to accept their new family too quickly they actually drove them further away.

When Julie and I got together we knew it was really important that we created a new family unit, including both mine and Julie's children from previous relationships. We made sure that we went out together as often as we could, creating memories and experiences for our new family. We expected our parents and friends to feel the same way, but while we had moved on from past relationships we now realise that they hadn't. My parents in particular were really upset that I had separated from my ex and still spent time with her. They kept asking for me to go and visit them on my own with their grandchildren but I didn't want to leave Julie and her kids out. I realise now that they just needed time to adjust but at the time I resented the way they seemed to be pushing Julie away. Our relationship was really distant for quite some time but thankfully now we all get on really well. If I could change anything it would be to let people adjust to the changes in their own time and not try and rush them until they're ready.

GREG, STEPDAD FOR FIVE YEARS TO TWO CHILDREN AGED TEN AND EIGHT

Friends will also need time – and help – in getting used to the changes in your family. Meeting up with friends may involve more planning. You may need to juggle two sets of children or have to consider the complexities of babysitters when previously you've just had to consider yourself. You may have weekends with your children and stepchildren and weekends without children. If possible, give your friends an option on whether they want child-friendly or child-free get-togethers.

Guidelines for extended family (grandparents, aunts, uncles, brothers, sisters, etc.)

➤ Make your stepchildren feel part of your family by including them in family parties and social events.

➤ Accept that there will be times when you can't see your grandchildren on their own and that your stepgrandchildren will be there also. Try and make them all feel welcome and special.

➤ Buy Christmas and birthday presents for stepchildren – even if they're just token presents – so that they feel included and accepted in the wider family.

➤ Make an effort to get to know stepchildren – their likes and dislikes, their favourite subjects at school or their hobbies.

➤ Don't be afraid to talk to your daughter/son/ sister/brother if you need a bit of help in understanding the new rules.

Guidelines for friends

➤ Be more flexible in your relationships with friends who are members of stepfamilies. Arrangements can be more complicated.

➤ Invite all members of the new family to get-togethers, even if they can't all make it. Treat the stepfamily as you would any other regular family.

Help your family and friends by setting the right tone as early as you can. So, for example, at Christmas make sure your Christmas cards are signed from everyone in the family – including your stepchildren (unless of course they're grown up with their own children). Get used to including your stepchildren in your family definition. For example, if someone asks how many children you have, don't miss them out, and get into the habit of talking about *all* the children – not just your biological children. The more you include your stepchildren in your family, the more others will take your lead. It's important that you recognise that particularly in the early days of a stepfamily it can be hard for your family and friends to know how to treat your new family. You need to help them and you need to give them time to adjust to the changes.

FAMILY MEETINGS

While part of your mission in creating a 'unified' stepfamily involves setting the right tone with your family and friends, the most critical part is in developing the framework within your own family. All families need their own rules and their own boundaries. And you might argue that since stepfamilies are often more complex than first families it's even *more* important to set down clear guidelines for everyone to follow. If there are clear boundaries it's far easier for parents and step-parents to be fair and consistent in the way they deal with all the children.

Depending on the age of your stepchildren it might be worth considering having regular 'family meetings' as a way of sharing news or rules or just making sure everyone has a voice. These meetings can be as formal or as informal as you like. You could choose to start a meeting over dinner, in the car or while you're out on a walk. The important thing is to provide an environment where everyone can participate and feel people listen to them. This can be particularly important for stepfamilies with non-residential stepchildren who may feel that they don't really belong in the family. By including them in your decisions and plans they will feel that they are an integral part of the family. Make sure everyone feels they can talk frankly to each other – about good things and bad. You should include any topic that affects the family, whether it's holiday plans, clarifying house rules, airing grievances or just saying sorry. As adults, you need to take charge of the meeting but make sure everyone has a voice and don't get intimidated by others. While it's important to encourage everyone to be open with their feelings you need to tread the line between being open and being hurtful.

MANAGING MEALTIMES

Mealtimes are a great way of creating special family time together and developing new family traditions. Whether you're together all the time or just some of the time try and use these times to sit down together and talk about what everyone's been doing that day or that week. We all lead busy lifestyles, and often work and other commitments can get in the way, but try and set aside time for family meals. Whether it's every Wednesday or every other Sunday, make an effort to share a meal, where you all sit down together as a family and share stories and update each other on what's going on in your lives. While it doesn't matter how elaborate the meal is try and make sure that it's something everyone is going to like. The aim of these shared mealtimes is to create happy times. Giving a toddler (or teenager!) a meal that they're going to pick at is only going to increase your stress levels, though if you can only sit down as a family once a week it's more important to concentrate on the topics of conversation rather than the food as such. Try and include everyone in the preparation so that they all feel as though they belong. Perhaps little ones can help set the table, while older children or teenagers might learn to appreciate being given extra responsibility and help to prepare the meal. Lots of children enjoy making cakes and biscuits and showing off their skills to the rest of the family. Make sure there aren't any distractions such as the television or mobile phones. In this way, you're reinforcing the importance of mealtimes together. If you can persevere, these times will quickly become new traditions that everyone can share in and enjoy.

HOUSEWORK

Unfortunately, while I wish it wasn't true, houses don't run themselves. No sooner have you cleaned the house from top to toe than it seems to need re-doing. No sooner have you emptied the laundry baskets and finished a dozen cycles in the washing machine than miraculously the baskets are full again. And the bigger the family, the more housework there is. Consequently, the arrival of your stepchildren is likely to have increased the daily chores as there are just more things to do.

Stepmums can come to resent the extra 'work' that comes with their stepchildren, which, after all, is rarely appreciated by them. This is all about getting the balance right. It's unfair that you should bear the brunt of all the extra workload but equally it's hardly fair to set your step-children to work the moment they walk through the door! If you find that you're beginning to resent the practical aspects of being a stepmum think about the changes you could start to make in your family, with the help of your partner and the children. Maybe you could set up a rota for some of the household duties or even cultivate an interest in cooking with older children. As long as you feel there's some sort of fairness it's up to you and your family to decide what works best in your household.

Lucy is 14 and lives with her mum and stepdad for most of the time, visiting her dad and his partner every other weekend. Her father used to live in the same town as Lucy but recently he moved to be with his partner. Their new house is just under an hour away. Lucy looks forward to seeing her dad but is finding it hard to get used to him living so much further away. When she does go to visit she feels as though she's 'in the way' all the time and doesn't know what to do. The last time she visited she had a 'lie in' in the morning – not unusual for teenagers, after all, but when she went downstairs her stepmother seemed cross. She told her that she had expected her to get up much earlier so that she could help tidy the house. Lucy was confused and angry. No one had explained what was expected of her in the house, but given the amount of time she was spending with her father and stepmother, Lucy didn't think it was fair to expect her to help with the housework. The problem was left to fester and just led to more resentment from Lucy and probably equal resentment from her stepmother.

In this case, Lucy, her father and her stepmother needed to set some rules and boundaries. If Lucy was expected to help out in the house then her dad and his partner needed to explain to Lucy what they wanted her to do. However, given the house move and the newness of the stepfamily it was probably too early for Lucy's stepmother to expect Lucy to do too much to help out.

The most important thing is to set the ground rules for all the children in your family – whether they are biological or stepchildren and whether they live full-time or only part-time in your household. The rules must be fair for everyone, so if you expect your own children to make their beds every morning then it's only fair to expect your stepchildren to do the same (assuming they're old enough). If you treat the children differently then this will only undermine your stepfamily. If for some reason you do have to treat them differently (for example, if your stepchildren are much younger than your children or vice versa) then make sure you explain this to your children clearly.

Take some time to work out with your partner what you expect everyone to contribute to the household, whether it's making their own beds, setting the table or putting their dirty clothes in the laundry basket. Be clear and consistent with all the children. It's important that both of you have an equal say in this area. If either of you is unhappy with the balance it's only likely to cause more resentment later.

Things to consider when making your household rules

➤ Have the confidence to tell your stepchildren what you expect them to do and remind them of their duties. Children have particularly bad memories for tasks that they don't enjoy.

➤ Be fair and consistent. Make sure that you apply the same rules to all the children. Don't be tempted to give in to one child. It'll only set a precedent, leading to resentment from the other children in the family.

➤ Be patient when you're establishing a routine. There's a fine line between persistence and nagging.

➤ Remember to praise them when they do a good job. Often it's too easy to tell children off for what they haven't done right and then forget to thank them or praise them when they do well.

> ➤ Try not to be too obsessive about tidiness. If you live for the majority of the time without children in your house it can be quite a shock to the system when your stepchildren come to stay. Perhaps you can learn to live with a bit of clutter while they're visiting as long as they tidy up before they leave? Or perhaps they could leave some things around in their room just not in the living rooms? It's important to make your stepchildren feel at home when they're with you and having their toys or possessions around may help them feel more comfortable.
>
> ➤ Don't expect them to read your mind. If you need help with something or want them to do something, just ask them. Don't fall into the trap of becoming resentful if they don't behave in a certain way.

Above all, be fair and reasonable. Think about the ages of your stepchildren and what they should or could help with. If you haven't got children of your own and aren't sure, talk to friends who have and ask them what they do. And finally, take things slowly. Don't expect changes overnight, but if you and your partner apply the rules consistently there's no reason why you can't turn things round so that you all share (even in a small way) in the running of the household.

CHILDCARE

One of the key things to agree between yourself and your partner is the level of childcare you are willing and able to carry out. While it's easy to be enthusiastic initially and help to look after your partner's children, it can easily lead to resentment from either or both of you if you aren't honest about the long-term role you want to play. Clare had been a stepmother for 10 years. In the early years she had played a huge part in looking after her stepdaughter when she came to stay but lately their relationship had become distant.

When I first moved in with Pete, his little girl was only two. She used to come and visit for weekends and I really loved seeing her. Pete had a really stressful job so he was tired at weekends and I wanted to help. We quickly settled into a routine with me providing the majority of the childcare. I would feed her, bathe her and put her to bed. I really enjoyed it at first. I loved her cuddles and began to feel really close to her. But over time, Pete started to take advantage. He would pick his daughter up and then arrange to go out with his friends. He'd ask if I minded and although I'd say no, I really did! Eventually, after one weekend where I felt like the hired help I told him that we needed to change things. He seemed to have forgotten that I wasn't his daughter's biological mum and that she was his responsibility. Things were quite difficult between us for a long time after that. I felt guilty that I didn't want to look after his daughter in the same way her mother would and he didn't quite know what he could and couldn't ask me to help with any more. It wasn't that I didn't want to help, I just didn't want to do everything.

CLARE, STEPMOTHER FOR 10 YEARS TO A 12-YEAR-OLD STEPDAUGHTER

Clare had fallen into the trap of setting unrealistic expectations for herself with her partner. Pete had assumed things would work the same as they had in his previous relationship. What he hadn't considered was the fact that Clare was not his daughter's mother. While she was willing to help him care for his daughter, the ultimate responsibility fell to him. However, once Clare and Pete had set some new ground rules they were able to work together on building their new family. Pete stopped automatically assuming that Clare would look after his daughter. Clare was of course happy to look after her stepdaughter but simply had resented being taken for granted.

While some step-parents take a real 'hands-on' approach to the job, others are happier, at least initially, to take more of a back seat and let their partner do the lion's share of the childcare. There are many different reasons for this and there is no right or wrong way to behave. For example, if your stepchildren are very young and you have no experience with children you may not feel confident enough to look after them on your own. Or you may have children of your own and find it difficult to look after your partner's children as well, without some support from him.

You need to take time to discuss this with your partner to make sure he understands how much help with his children you're willing and able to give. Make sure you're honest with your partner – and yourself. It's fine to admit that you feel out of your depth or feel nervous about looking after them, or simply that you need a break from time to time when they're around. Just be clear about the help you're willing to give so that you both have realistic expectations. If your partner is expecting you to cook dinner for everyone when he arrives home with his children and you've arranged to go out with friends, it's likely that he will feel disappointed and let down. By letting your partner know how much support he can expect from you, you can hopefully avoid this type of problem. Of course, it may be that over time as you all get used to your new family and your confidence grows, you'll be happier sharing more of the childcare responsibilities. If it's an injection of confidence you need, make sure your partner supports you so that in turn you can support him.

DISCIPLINE

This is one of the more sensitive issues for step-parents to deal with. Should they discipline their stepchildren or should they leave it to their partners? If they do discipline them, what is an appropriate punishment? What if their step-children don't accept being disciplined from them? It's a minefield that step-parents have to negotiate from the moment they take on the role.

One stepmother, Eve, recounted a story where she had been looking after her seven-year-old stepdaughter.

My partner was working away from home and wasn't due to return until the morning. During the evening my stepdaughter had been naughty and I had had to tell her off. She said 'you're not my mummy, you can't tell me off'. I calmly told her that, no, I wasn't her mummy but that I was in charge and would tell her off if she was naughty. But she refused to calm down and just kept repeating I wasn't allowed to tell her off.

Eventually, at the end of my tether, I told her that I was going to take her home so that she could explain to her mummy why she had been naughty. This shocked her and she apologised and eventually calmed down.

EVE, STEPMUM FOR FIVE YEARS TO STEPDAUGHTER
AGED SEVEN

Clearly, in this example, Eve had been left as the sole carer for her stepdaughter and needed to be the disciplinarian. But no one had made it clear to Eve's stepdaughter that Eve was in charge.

It's very difficult in the early days of a stepfamily for step-parents to enforce discipline in their stepchildren. Research shows that it's much better if the step-parent avoids getting involved in discipline issues initially but concentrates on getting to know their stepchildren and gaining their respect and trust. Only then will they be in a position to enforce discipline if it's needed. That's not to say that they can't enforce house rules though, but serious disciplinary matters are often best left to the biological parent, at least at the beginning of the relationship.

However, if you are left in sole care of your step-children it's perfectly reasonable to both enforce rules and dish out discipline if needed. Make sure that you and your partner talk about how you both want to handle this issue. Once you do get involved in disciplining your stepchildren make sure your partner supports any decisions you make and that you're consistent in disciplining all the children in your family.

FAMILY CELEBRATIONS

Family celebrations, such as birthdays, weddings, christenings, graduation or Christmas, are highlights for any family and provide a chance to get together and enjoy time with family and friends. But for stepfamilies these celebrations can also bring pangs of jealousy and envy for longed-for 'normality' as these events often have to be shared in some way with the other biological parent. This can leave the step-parent feeling isolated. It's important to be flexible at these times, to accommodate for the added complications of stepfamily life.

CELEBRATION SCENARIOS

Read through these scenarios and work out what you think you would do in each case.

1. Your five-year-old stepdaughter is having a birthday party. Her mother has arranged it but your partner has contributed to the costs. Your partner is going to the party and he wants you to go with him but you know his ex won't want you there.
2. Your stepson has his graduation ceremony planned and has invited his mother and father. You really want to attend and feel sure that he could get another ticket but your partner seems to be reluctant to ask.
3. Christmas is fast approaching and you're looking forward to your first Christmas together. Unfortunately, your partner's ex wants the children to spend Christmas Day with her. You know your partner is really upset but you don't know what to do to help.

4. Your adult stepdaughter is getting married next year. You have known her since she was a teenager and really want to be at the ceremony; however, you have never got on with your partner's ex and you're really worried that you won't be welcome. Your partner doesn't want to go without you but obviously wants to be there for his daughter.

Scenario 1

Children's birthdays can become extremely emotive issues. They're very special times for children and it's only natural to want to be part of the celebrations. Sometimes it's easy to get caught up in the issues between the adults and lose sight of the person that really matters, in this case the birthday girl. In a perfect world it would be ideal if all three adults could attend the party and feel part of the celebrations but sometimes past feelings and relationships can get in the way. In this scenario there's certainly no harm in the partner asking his ex if she would be happy if his new partner could attend – as long as this wouldn't be stressful for the little girl. Alternatively, why not consider having a separate celebration for her birthday, where you can invite other family and friends.

Scenario 2

It's time to put aside your own feelings and consider your stepson. This is his day and one he's been working towards for a long time. It's only natural that he will want both his parents there to share in his day. If there is no animosity between the biological mother and the stepmother then there's no reason why all three parents couldn't attend but the most important person to consider here is your stepson and his feelings. In this scenario, the stepmother should talk to her partner to understand why he is reluctant for her to attend – it may be that he is worried about somehow spoiling the day for his son if there is an atmosphere between the parents.

Scenario 3

Christmas time can bring home one of the hardest things stepfamilies have to deal with – having to 'share' your children. For part-time stepfamilies, who live their lives with children shuttling to and fro between their homes, by and large this works well. It's only when we reach immovable dates such as Christmas or birthdays that sharing becomes much more difficult. There is only one Christmas Day and the general consensus is that Father Christmas will only deliver presents on Christmas Eve. This makes it difficult to agree on Christmas arrangements for most stepfamilies with young children as obviously both biological parents don't want to miss out. However, rather than dwell on one special day, as a stepfamily you need to try and come up with alternatives. Find your own traditions.

A friend of mine, for example, always celebrates Christmas with her children on Christmas Eve. The presents 'arrive' early before they go to bed. The children then spend Christmas Day with their father and his partner, while my friend enjoys a more grown-up Christmas Day with her friends and family. Another alternative is to alternate Christmas Day and Boxing Day. So one year you have all the children on Christmas Day and have a 'normal' Christmas. The next year you have Christmas Day on your own where you can indulge in plenty of food and wine and then the children come back for Boxing Day, when you can all share presents and have a second Christmas together.

It's really a state of mind. It's about learning to dwell on what you have got – not what you *haven't* got. In this scenario the stepmum needs to reassure her partner that they can celebrate their Christmas Day when his children come to visit – whether that's Boxing Day or 29th December. It doesn't matter as long as you adopt the right approach. However, it's worth spending time planning your arrangements for the children over Christmas. You need to make sure everyone's clear about each other's plans so that no one is disappointed at the last minute.

Scenario 4
Weddings are a time to put aside your own personal feelings and think about your stepchild and their partner. This is their day and I'm sure they will be trying to consider everyone's feelings as well as their own. It's important to talk to your stepdaughter and reassure her that you'll understand whatever decision she comes to. Obviously let them know that you dearly want to share in their day but that you will understand whatever they decide. If it's difficult for you to attend the actual event then try and find a way to be part of the celebrations in some other way, whether it's a special meal together before the wedding or a even a party when they return from their honeymoon.

All family celebrations are ways of creating and reinforcing family traditions. Use these times to create your own memories with your new family. Make sure that as far as possible, everyone is included in family birthdays and Christmas celebrations. If your stepchildren arrive after you've celebrated your Christmas Day and opened all your presents they're likely to feel left out and not really part of the family. However, if you all have Christmas dinner together, every year at 2 p.m., wearing silly hats from the crackers with Dad/Stepdad carving the turkey, it doesn't matter whether this happens on Christmas Day or any other day. This will be *your* special Christmas Day.

It's also worth considering how you want to deal with presents in the family. This can be a contentious issue with some people holding strong views about the importance of separating presents from parents and step-parents. My own view is that this is an opportunity to show your children and stepchildren that you are a couple and you are all part of a family. Consider sending presents jointly from you and your partner to all the children for their birthdays and Christmases and make sure they send each other presents – even if they need a little help in funding and choosing!

HOLIDAYS

We went on our first family holiday last year and it was the worst experience of my life. We took my two stepchildren to France for 10 days and I found the whole experience a nightmare. There was nowhere to escape to. We were all sharing a family room as the children were too young to have their own room so I had no privacy. And my husband seemed to indulge them all the time. In the end I resorted to locking myself in the toilet to have a good cry on my own. My husband thought it was the best holiday ever and I think my stepchildren enjoyed it but I'm just dreading another one.

HELEN, STEPMUM FOR THREE YEARS TO TWO
STEPCHILDREN AGED NINE AND SIX

Helen found that she just wasn't prepared for the family holiday. As a part-time stepmum she wasn't used to having her stepchildren around all the time and found the transition difficult to handle. In hindsight she could have perhaps suggested a short break or weekend away with her partner and stepchildren to 'test the water', before embarking on a long holiday together. And while sharing a room is the easiest solution for families with young children it's not necessarily the best option for everyone. If Helen had booked an apartment rather than a hotel she would at least have had some privacy with her partner. The extra cost might just have been worth it! A friend of mine made the mistake of trying to force everyone together very early in their relationship. She and her partner planned a bucket-and-spade seaside holiday with her children and her partner's children. They also invited the grandparents thinking it would be a great opportunity for everyone to get to know one another. Unfortunately, it was a disaster and not something she will be repeating in a hurry. They hadn't talked properly before the holiday and as no one knew what the rules were they spent the entire week joined at the hip to everyone else. Everyone tried to be polite but it was awkward and difficult.

Holidays are precious. For those stepmums who work full-time, there are only so many weeks in the year where you can take a break and relax so there is huge pressure to really enjoy those times. However, if you're used to adult-only holidays, taking a break with your stepchildren can be a real shock to the system. Your time is no longer just your own and you have to consider keeping everyone happy and entertained. But while these may be the downsides of step-family holidays there are plenty of upsides! A holiday is a great time to get to know each other and relax and enjoy each other's company. As always, it's about keeping realistic expectations and being clear with your partner about what you each want from the holiday.

A holiday has to be just that – a holiday for everyone. Try and find somewhere that is likely to offer something you will all enjoy. A remote beach holiday may be your idea of bliss but if there's nothing for the children to do you will turn into chief children's entertainer – probably not your ideal of a relaxing holiday. Similarly, a fortnight in Disney World is probably not your idea of bliss but would be paradise for most children. Try and find a com-promise that offers things for the children to do while giving you and your partner some time to yourselves. Obviously if the children are very young this can be almost impossible, so be realistic.

If possible always try and find accommodation where you and your partner have a room to yourselves. It's import-ant that you have some privacy to talk about any worries you might have or just to let off steam. As Helen found, it can be difficult when you have nowhere to escape to.

Holidays are a great way of building memories for all families and are a really important way to integrate your stepfamily, but take things slowly. Maybe try a long weekend break first to see how things go. Talk to your partner about what you want from a holiday. It's important that everyone – including you and your partner – enjoys themselves.

Your aim should be to create a new family identity for your stepfamily, distinct from any previous family groups. This new identity has to be driven by you and your partner. You both need to take the lead in creating the household rules and traditions for your new family. Without these your family is likely to remain two parts of disparate biological families, driven by different rules and expectations. Work with your partner to develop the way you want your family to run. Children need guidance on what they're expected to do. If they don't set the table when they're with their biological mother then they're not automatically going to think about it when they're with you. That doesn't mean they're thoughtless, it's just not part of their routine. It's up to you to create the routine in your household.

But while it's critical that you develop a family identity with your partner and children, it's equally important that you help your family and friends to know what to expect. They may not understand the complications of stepfamily life so it's up to you to explain it to them so that they can understand and help.

However, none of this happens overnight. You need to give everyone plenty of time to get used to the changes and adjust their behaviour. As I've said, you and your partner are at the centre of your family and above all you mustn't let anything come between you. Keep talking to each other and keep listening. Biological parents and step-parents can have very different views, driven by inherently different perspectives. Try to understand and support your partner and ask them to do the same for you.

And finally, be patient. Stepfamilies take time to work things out. If your first Christmas is a disaster or your family holiday a nightmare, just try and learn from it. What did you do wrong? What could you have changed? Don't give up. You're with your partner because you love them and, between you, you can build a strong stepfamily if you give yourselves the chance to learn together.

5

Learning How to Cope
More Effectively

Despite the many challenges stepmothers and stepfamilies face, the majority of us manage to emerge relatively unscathed and above all happy and at ease in our families. And while it's good to understand the types of problems we might encounter as stepmums, it's worth putting things into perspective. Yes, there are difficulties – but *all* couples and families have to deal with difficult problems from time to time. Rather than always focusing on the differences between stepfamilies and first families and wishing for something that you can't have, concentrate on the positives in your relationship with your partner and in your stepfamily.

The trick is to learn to have confidence in your abilities to be the best stepmum you can, and how to be content and happy in your role. Becoming comfortable in your role doesn't happen overnight: it takes time for everyone to get to know one another and for you to carve out your role in the family. There are a series of stages that many stepfamilies pass through as they develop. While these stages are not hard and fast they do give you an indication of where you are in your family development. By understanding these stages, you can understand more clearly why you're experiencing the feelings and emotions you do and how to move through the stages more effectively.

We each have different ways of dealing with stressful situations – with some ways more effective than others! By learning to recognise the difference between positive and negative coping mechanisms – and identifying which coping mechanism you tend to rely on when dealing with stress – it's possible to develop more effective ways of dealing with conflict, leading to better outcomes – for you and your family.

TIME – THE GREAT HEALER

Remember, becoming a confident and happy stepmum doesn't happen instantly – stepfamilies take time to develop and grow into successful family units. The first years can be difficult for stepfamilies – as they can for most couples starting out in a new relationship. The difference for step-families is that there are more relationships to consider from day 1. It's not just the couple who have to get used to living with each other: the adults need to get used to living with each other and their respective children, not to mention the involvement of ex-partners. Not surprisingly, it can be quite a shock to the system.

It's in the first two years, when no one is clear about the rules in the family or understands their roles, when things are tricky. This is often thought of as a time of turbulence and disorganisation and is perfectly normal. However, over time, everyone learns to adjust to the changes. This is where as a stepmum, you've defined your role in the family, and you've got to know your stepchildren and built a relationship with them based on trust and respect. If you've built the right foundations there's no reason why you can't continue along this path and put behind you the early problems. However, it's equally possible that the changes you've put into place cause different problems, which mean you have to revisit the turbulent times. Sometimes these things are out of our control, your stepchildren may move house, meaning that your access with them changes, there may be financial problems or your stepchildren turn into nightmare teenagers. I'm afraid this is just part of life and, difficult as it can be, we just have to learn to cope with whatever it throws at us.

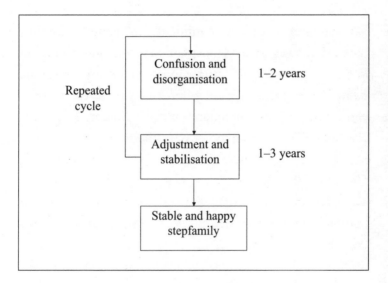

STAGES OF STEPFAMILY DEVELOPMENT

Most stepfamilies go through predictable stages as they learn to live together as a family. By understanding these stages it can help you understand why you might feel the way you do now and what to expect in the future, so that you can be better prepared and ready to cope more effectively. Progression from one stage to the next depends on meeting the challenges of the previous stage.

THE HONEYMOON PERIOD

This is when you and your partner meet and fall in love. You may have fantasised about rescuing each other and his children from a sad past, perhaps even protecting your partner from their previous partner. But while you may fantasise that your partner's children will welcome you as a new stepmum, the children may cling to the hope that their parents will get back together or that you will disappear. While this stage can't last for ever it's an important and natural part of the stepfamily development. As time passes, you will begin to get to know your new family, and they you, and hopefully move on to the next phase.

FACING REALITY

You are now accepted as the new stepmum and you've become family to your stepchildren. However, in many ways you are still an outsider. You may feel left out of the family unit or even rejected by the stepchildren, leading to resentment and confusion about the way you feel. You may take a step back from family life in an effort to somehow shield yourself from further hurt – which may in turn be interpreted as a lack of desire to be part of the family by your partner. Once you recognise these feelings and decide to change things, you're ready to move forward to the next stage of development.

RECOGNISING THE NEED FOR CHANGE

By now you've identified the problems within your family. You now know that there need to be changes but you don't know how to fix them. Often this is the stage at which many stepmums start to look for help, maybe from others in the same position or from articles or books. You need to find reassurance that your feelings are 'normal' and part of the process, as well as finding help in addressing the issues that have caused the problems in your new family.

A PROBLEM SHARED

This is the time to start being honest with your partner and talk to him about the way you feel and the changes you want to happen in the family. While both adults can initiate this stage it's usually the step-parent who's pressing for the changes in order to be a more equal partner and member of the family. There's often much negotiation and even conflict in this stage but it's important to talk through the issues if your new family is to move forward. The issues can affect many areas of family life such as contact with previous partners, finance or maintenance payments, contact arrangements and disciplining the children.

WORKING TOGETHER

Once you've aired the problems with your partner and you both understand the issues it's vital that you work together to resolve them. As you start to take decisions together, whether it's disciplining the children or creating your own household rules, you're taking the first steps in becoming a more integrated, happier family unit. This process will take a while.

It's likely that the issues were festering some time before you recognised the problem so it will take time for the feelings of isolation, hurt, anger or jealousy to subside. So you need to be patient and keep working together with your partner.

RESOLUTION AND ACCEPTANCE

This is the point where the stepfamily have learned to deal with any problems they had between them. They feel more confident and able to cope with whatever life throws at them. Their stepfamily will have developed its own ways and rituals that define it uniquely and their relationships with each other are solid and reliable.

Although these stages may appear 'cut and dried', they usually merge into one another without the family being aware of the change. It's only with the benefit of hindsight that you notice the changes in the relationship. Some families take longer than others to move through the stages and although there is no hard and fast rule, it's typical for a family to take several years to progress to the final phase.

Take some time to look through the phases and work out where you think you are in the cycle. Remember, each stage is essential to the development of any stepfamily – the important part is to not get trapped in any one stage for too long.

COPING STRATEGIES

How do you cope with problems? Do you tend to bury your head in the sand or do you set to work to find a solution as quickly as possible? Take a moment to answer the following questionnaire as honestly as you can. If you feel you agree with the statement and this reflects how you *often* deal with a difficult problem, then you have a tendency to use the coping style indicated.

How I tend to cope with problems . . .	Coping style
I daydream about things to take my mind off the reality	Disengaged
I've accepted the situation and that it can't be changed	Accepting
I think about the best way to handle a problem	Planning
I try to get advice from someone who has experienced similar problems	Seek support
I go to the cinema or watch TV so that I don't have to think about the problems	Disengaged
I try to see things in a different light, to make it seem more positive	Positive mindset
I've realised that I can't deal with things so I've stopped trying	Disengaged
I've learned to live with things as they are	Accepting
I do what has to be done, one step at a time	Planning
I try to learn from my experiences and look forward positively	Positive mindset
I've stopped putting in as much effort into solving the problems as I know I'm not going to win	Disengaged
I try to talk to someone about how I feel	Seek support

Disengaged

I don't get on with my stepchildren. I've tried, but things just don't seem to get any better. I may as well just keep out of their way in future. When they come to visit I'll just make my excuses and go out. That way we won't have to see each other and I won't be stressed any more.

The disengaged coping style is all about doing anything to divert attention from the problem in hand, whether that's watching the TV or just daydreaming about what life could be like. At the extreme, it's about giving up and feeling overwhelmed by the problem. Although it can be harmless in small doses – after all we all want to escape from reality at times – it doesn't help fix anything in the long term and can lead to more anxiety and even depression as the problems become more ingrained. If you find that you tend to react like this in a crisis, try and make a conscious effort to reduce your reliance on it and think about using some of the other coping methods described below.

Accepting

While I wish we didn't have all the added complications of being a stepfamily, that's what we are. My partner's children are a really important part of his life and therefore my life. It would be great not to have to deal with his ex but that's just the way it is. Nothing's perfect – we'll just make things work for us as well as we can.

Sometimes it's necessary simply to accept a situation and recognise that it can't be changed. This often happens when people are trying to cope with a bereavement or illness. For stepfamilies it's usually related to individuals accepting that they are fundamentally different from biological families and adopting more realistic expectations. Acceptance is therefore an essential coping style for some situations and can be used on its own or with other styles, such as seeking support or adopting a positive mindset. Learning to use this coping style to face issues can help reduce your anxiety and stress.

Planning

I have a really good relationship with my eldest stepson but the younger two seem to just ignore me and show me no respect. I've spoken to my partner and we really need to try and improve things. I'm going to try and rope my eldest stepson in to help. I'm sure he will appreciate me putting my trust in him and hopefully he can help persuade his brothers to get on with me better and make them realise that I'm not trying to replace their mum but just want to get to know them better.

This coping style is concerned with thinking about how to cope with a stressful situation. It's about coming up with strategies, about what steps to take and how best to handle the problem. It's about taking some control and dealing with the matter. However, if you're struggling to cope, sometimes it can be difficult to see a way forward. If this is the case, try and talk to a close friend or relative to come up with possible solutions. Adopting this approach is much more effective in the long term and is a much healthier way forward than disengaging from the issues.

Positive mindset

My partner is really sad that he can't spend Christmas with his children this year as his ex is taking them away for the holidays. While I know he's really disappointed I've arranged for us to have a special 'Christmas Day' with them before they leave, with Christmas dinner and presents and the tree, and I've booked us into a really nice hotel for Christmas Day, just the two of us. I know he'd rather have a family Christmas but at least this way he gets to have a special day with his children and a very different celebration in the hotel with me, which won't remind him of our usual Christmases.

This coping style is aimed at managing the distress from a situation rather than changing it – in a similar way to acceptance. However, as it also concentrates on making the best of a situation, it's well suited to stepfamily dynamics where there are often situations that can't be altered but can be turned into positives. For example, you might not have the greatest relationship with your stepchildren, but you have a loving partner and things are generally improving. Learn to build on the positives and not look for the negatives. In this way you adopt a much more positive approach to the way you view problems which can help lower your stress.

Seek support

> I'm really fed up with everything. My partner doesn't realise how difficult it is for me when his children come to stay. I don't have my own children so I just don't feel very confident with them. I really enjoy talking to my friend. She always helps me work through the problems and helps me see things more clearly. Sometimes it's easier talking to someone who's one step removed from the family – they're not so emotionally involved and can usually see things a bit more rationally!

Individuals seek social support for advice or information – such as whether a Chicken Jalfrezi is the best choice of meals for a three-year-old! – or moral support and sympathy, seeking a shoulder to cry on and share their problems. Although both these types of support are generally positive, take care not to become over-reliant on 'tea and sympathy'. Sometimes it's great just to be able to offload our problems to friends and whinge about whatever is annoying us but try and make sure you balance this with talking about how to try and make things better rather than simply concentrating on them giving you a sympathetic ear! It'll be more effective in the long run.

MANAGING YOUR STYLE

We all rely on different coping styles at different times and for different situations. Sometimes we recognise that a situation won't change and we have to learn to accept the outcome and move on; other times we need to find solutions to a problem or adopt a 'glass half full' approach. It's important that we learn to use different coping styles at different times as this can really help manage our stress and anxiety. If you feel that you're avoiding dealing with issues and relying too heavily on the 'disengaging' form of coping, take a few minutes to look at the alternative coping styles. Think about a recent problem you've had and try and come up with alternative ways that you could have dealt with the problem. The following example might give you some ideas.

Alison had moved in with her partner a year earlier. She didn't have any children of her own but her partner had two young children aged five and seven years old from a previous relationship who came to visit every other weekend. They had talked about this before Alison had moved in but she hadn't been worried as she had plenty of nephews and nieces and really liked having children around. But once she moved in she found things were very different from how she'd imagined. Rather than look forward to the children coming to stay she found herself resenting them. She resented the way they seemed to just take over for the weekend. The children just wanted to be with their dad and she felt like a spare part. Over time her feelings got worse. She found herself getting anxious in the days leading up to the weekend, wondering what they would do and how she could make excuses to escape.

When I spoke to Alison about her behaviour she realised that it couldn't continue. It was making her feel miserable for most of the time and her partner was becoming very frustrated. He couldn't understand why it was such a big deal to her and just expected her to enjoy the weekends when they were all together. Over the next few weeks Alison began to make some changes to help her cope with the situation. She spent some time talking to her partner and explained that although she found it difficult she was going to try harder but wanted his help. She began by accepting that her stepchildren were part of her life now and weekends would always involve them. She agreed with her partner that they would make more effort to plan the weekends with the children so that they all did a family activity or outing together, whether that was going to the pictures or a walk in the park. But as part of the weekend Alison would also get to spend some time with friends so that she had time on her own. As the weeks passed Alison found that she was becoming less anxious about the weekends and the children seemed to be more relaxed.

At the beginning of the relationship Alison was coping with the situation by simply not acknowledging it. She didn't want to deal with the fact that her stepchildren were coming to stay and did all she could to just stay out of their way. But this couldn't last for ever if her relationship was to continue with her partner. Alison was able to change the way she was coping with the problem by firstly accepting the situation and then putting a plan of action into place, with the support of her partner. Over time this led to Alison being much more relaxed and happy in her new relationship and with her new stepfamily.

If you recognise something of yourself and your own circumstances in the way Alison felt, think about whether it's time to change the way you approach your relationship with your stepchildren or other aspects of family life. If you're relying on the 'disengaged' type of coping style think about how you might adopt more positive approaches to become a happier stepmum.

Becoming part of a stepfamily and a stepmum isn't a walk in the park. As any woman who has had children of her own will tell you, children bring a certain level of stress to any relationship, and that's when you've had time to live with your partner on your own prior to the arrival of the little ones. Stepfamilies are thrown together and somehow need to untangle the complicated web of relationships and feelings. Many stepfamilies develop into successful and happy family units.

Top tips from successful stepmums

➤ Accept that conflict is healthy and part of normal, loving relationships.

➤ Be honest and open. Learn to listen without criticising.

➤ Forge a relationship with your stepchildren based on mutual trust. Learn to like your stepchildren – love will come later.

➤ Say sorry! Learn to accept when you're wrong or simply need more help.

➤ Clarify your role in the family with all the other family members – remove any ambiguity.

➤ Learn to communicate effectively and resolve conflict – never go to bed angry!

> ➤ Spend quality time together as a family – have fun and make your own shared memories and create rituals that bind you together as a family unit.

> ➤ Make sure you can rely on a strong support system from family and friends as well as your partner.

> ➤ Try and find a positive relationship with the ex-partner – you don't have to be her best friend but a relationship without animosity can help.

> ➤ Have realistic expectations and don't try and rush things.

> ➤ Be flexible. Stepfamilies are more complicated than first families.

> ➤ Use your sense of humour. When all else fails, use humour to get you through!

Learn to like your family, spend time together and have fun! Above all make sure you keep talking to each other. Often it's easier to bottle things up and just hope the problem goes away, but this approach rarely works in the long term. Learn to face the problems together with your partner. If you're finding it hard to get on with your stepchildren, talk to your partner about what you can do to change things. Take some time to think about where you are in terms of the stepfamily cycle. Perhaps you've got stuck in one of the stages and need to make some changes to move forward. Put a plan into place. Work out what you need to change and talk it through with your partner. Think about how you cope with problems. Are you generally positive or do you tend to bury your head in the sand? It's time to raise your head above the parapet and take back control in your life.

6

The Importance of Support from Family and Friends

We all need help from time to time. Whether it's a free baby-sitting service from your mum, a chance to offload to your friends over a glass of wine or two, or persuading your partner to crack on with the list of DIY tasks he's been promising to get on with for the last six months! Whether it's emotional or practical support we need, we all rely on our family and friends in a whole manner of different ways every single day.

Support from our family and friends is essential to our daily life – but more than this it's recognised that the more support you have the better your psychological well-being. If you have a good social support structure you are less likely to suffer from depressive symptoms, you will have higher self-esteem and self-worth and be happier and more content with your life. In addition to psychological health, social support has also been shown to be linked to better physical health. Being able to rely on a wide circle of family and friends can be thought of as a 'buffer' against stress, anxiety and depression, helping us cope better with the problems that life throws at us. And while it's important to be able to rely on our partners for support, it's equally important that they are not our only shoulder to lean on.

Other family members, such as parents, brothers, sisters and even adult children, are also important to our social support network, as are our friends. For example, if you find it hard to talk to your partner about a particular subject it might be easier to turn to a friend who is less involved and can remain emotionally distant. Perhaps not surprisingly women typically have larger and more diverse social networks than men. However, women find it much harder than men to cope when they haven't got a strong support network.

Not surprisingly, research specifically on stepfamilies has shown that this kind of support is essential for stepmothers in developing 'successful' stepfamilies, while a lack of such support means that their relationships with their partners are likely to be less happy.

So the bottom line is that we all want – and need – support from our partner, our families and our friends. This is likely to make us feel better about ourselves and help us cope with day-to-day problems. But if we can't rely on this support what can we do to protect ourselves? If social support acts as a buffer against stress what can we do to bolster our protection?

HOW GOOD IS YOUR SOCIAL SUPPORT NETWORK?

Can you rely on the support of your friends when things get tough or do they find it hard to know what to say to you? Is your partner sympathetic to your problems or does he find it hard to understand your point of view? Take a few minutes to work out how good your own social support network is. Please take a moment to respond to the following statements as honestly as you can and add up your total at the end using the scores provided.

Support from your partner

1. I can rely on my partner to be there for me when I need him.

Strongly disagree	*1*
Disagree	*2*
Neither agree nor disagree	*3*
Agree	*4*
Strongly agree	*5*

2. I feel I can share everything with my partner – both good and bad.

Strongly disagree	*1*
Disagree	*2*
Neither agree nor disagree	*3*
Agree	*4*
Strongly agree	*5*

3. My partner is a real source of comfort to me.

Strongly disagree	*1*
Disagree	*2*
Neither agree nor disagree	*3*
Agree	*4*
Strongly agree	*5*

4. My partner really cares about my feelings.

Strongly disagree	*1*
Disagree	*2*
Neither agree nor disagree	*3*
Agree	*4*
Strongly agree	*5*

Support from your family members

5. My family (parents, in-laws, brothers, sisters, etc.) really try to help me.

Strongly disagree	*1*
Disagree	*2*
Neither agree nor disagree	*3*
Agree	*4*
Strongly agree	*5*

6. I get the emotional help and support I need from my family.

Strongly disagree	*1*
Disagree	*2*
Neither agree nor disagree	*3*
Agree	*4*
Strongly agree	*5*

7. I can talk about my problems with my family.

Strongly disagree	*1*
Disagree	*2*
Neither agree nor disagree	*3*
Agree	*4*
Strongly agree	*5*

8. I can always rely on my family to help me make difficult decisions.

Strongly disagree	*1*
Disagree	*2*
Neither agree nor disagree	*3*
Agree	*4*
Strongly agree	*5*

Support from your friends

9. My friends really try and help me.

Strongly disagree	*1*
Disagree	*2*
Neither agree nor disagree	*3*
Agree	*4*
Strongly agree	*5*

10. I can count on my friends when things go wrong.

Strongly disagree	*1*
Disagree	*2*
Neither agree nor disagree	*3*
Agree	*4*
Strongly agree	*5*

11. My friends understand and help me through good times and bad.

Strongly disagree	*1*
Disagree	*2*
Neither agree nor disagree	*3*
Agree	*4*
Strongly agree	*5*

12. I can talk about my problems with my friends.

Strongly disagree	*1*
Disagree	*2*
Neither agree nor disagree	*3*
Agree	*4*
Strongly agree	*5*

The first four statements relate to the support you get from your partner. Add up each of the four scores.

Now repeat this for statements 5–8, which relate to the support you get from your family; and finally for statements 9–12, which relate to the support you get from your friends.

You should now have a score for the support you receive from your partner, from your wider family and from your friends. Each of these three separate scores should be between 20 and 4, with a higher score reflecting more support.

Score

4–9   This score reflects very little support. It's really important to our well-being that we can rely on different sources of help, from our partner, family and friends. Following in this chapter are some ideas to boost the help or support you can rely on here.

10–14 You clearly get some support but it's far from ideal. Avoid the temptation to ignore this particular aspect of your support network and work out what you could change to improve things.

15–20 This score suggests you can really rely on support from this area in your life. Don't underestimate how much this helps you cope on a daily basis. Remember to show your appreciation!

If you scored 15 or above in all three areas, you obviously have a good network of support and can rely on these individuals to help you when you need it. However, if you scored lower in any of the three areas then this might suggest that you struggle to feel you can rely on this area of support.

The following section looks at each type of support in terms of the typical problems you may face and provides tips on how to improve these relationships, to give you the support you need and hopefully improve your well-being and happiness.

YOUR RELATIONSHIP WITH YOUR PARTNER

Needless to say, your relationship with your partner is pivotal to your overall well-being. As discussed in Chapter 2, the relationship you develop with your partner underpins your whole family, as without a strong partnership your stepfamily is unlikely to thrive no matter how much you each love the children in the family. So it's vital that you can truly count on your partner to give you the support you need. But if you're finding it hard to talk to your partner or turn to them for support take some time to work out why. Perhaps you tried talking to them in the past but things always seemed to be worse afterwards, with discussions quickly escalating into arguments. Or maybe he becomes defensive whenever you raise a problem and you want to avoid any confrontations. Whatever the reasons it's important that you recognise them and jointly try and work through them.

How to get the right support from your partner

➤ Don't dwell on things. If you're worried about something it's far better to talk about it than leave it unsaid. Try and talk to your partner rather than someone else if it's directly related to your stepfamily, such as your stepchildren's behaviour or working out the rules within your family. Others can sympathise and even advise, but don't have the power to change anything.

➤ Don't fall into the trap of making assumptions – find out the facts first.

➤ Don't be tempted to take out your frustrations on your partner just because they're the closest to you.

➤ Concentrate on one problem at a time.

➤ Don't blame everything that goes wrong in your family on being a stepfamily. Biological families have problems too!

➤ Accept that sometimes things will annoy or frustrate you and you'll need to let off steam. It might be that there's nothing you or your partner can do about it – but talking about it makes you feel better. Acknowledge this and let your partner know that you just want them to listen to you – not fix anything!

➤ Make sure you get a balance between focusing on problems and enjoying the good times. Every family has to deal with issues from time to time, and often,

> the more complicated the family, the more
> complicated the issues.

➤ Give yourselves a break. Enjoy time together and
  concentrate on making great memories, because
  these will help keep you going through difficult times.

However, our partner only provides one important 'leg' of our support system, with the other main support being derived from other family members and the third support from our friends. These three support mechanisms should balance each other, providing different types of support as and when we need it. While it's natural to turn to our partner for help and reassurance, sometimes we need a different perspective or advice from someone who's a step removed from the problem.

YOUR RELATIONSHIP WITH YOUR 'FAMILY'

The definition of 'family' can be quite confusing and can mean different things to different people. While one person can think of their family in terms of simple biological relatedness, others can adopt a more inclusive definition. However, when we're talking about the effect of social support it's important to think of the wider implications of 'family', as each individual within your wider family circle possesses the opportunity to have a positive or negative effect on your well-being and that of your stepfamily. So, for example, if your sister doesn't get on with your new partner, you'll be less likely to confide in her when you need help, or if your parents disapprove of your new relationship, it's hard to call on them to help with the babysitting.

YOUR SIBLINGS

Julia had been a stepmother for 10 years. She has one 17-year-old stepdaughter whom she is very close to, but no children of her own, and has managed to forge a relationship with her stepdaughter's mother for the benefit of her stepdaughter and partner. Her own parents have welcomed Julia's stepdaughter into the family and treat her as they would their own granddaughter. However, Julia's brother has never made her stepdaughter feel welcome and this has driven a wedge between them. Julia feels that he doesn't treat her stepdaughter in the same way that she treats his children. He has never bought her a birthday present and her Christmas present always seems like a token gift. In contrast Julia felt she carefully chose gifts that she knew her brother's children would like and appreciate. Julia resents her brother's lack of affection for her stepdaughter but then feels guilty for putting such weight on gifts in this way. This unspoken resentment means that whereas in the past she had relied on her brother for advice and support she now doesn't feel comfortable asking for his help.

While Julia interpreted her brother's lack of present buying as proof that he didn't accept her stepdaughter as truly part of their family, she realised that she had made quite a few assumptions based on very little evidence. The fact that he didn't buy her stepdaughter expensive presents may be more to do with forgetfulness or maybe simply a lack of cash than anything more sinister. When I asked her if he remembered other family members' birthdays she did agree that perhaps he wasn't the most reliable.

It's easy to fall into the trap of attributing all behaviour to the fact you're part of a stepfamily, without first trying to look at alternative causes. Often we try and fit the pieces of a puzzle together when they actually don't belong together. In Julia's case, she wanted everyone to accept her step-daughter into her family – as she had done – and was looking for signs of reassurance. The fact that her brother didn't choose and send presents with the same care she did was evidence to Julia that he didn't truly accept her step-daughter. In reality, her brother probably needed a bit of guidance in this area. Perhaps Julia could have started dropping hints of things that her stepdaughter might like to receive for her birthday and Christmas. If she'd had a close relationship with him, she could have tried the more direct approach and told her brother how she felt about her stepdaughter and that she would like everyone to treat her as part of the family.

As we've already discussed, the lack of recognised rules surrounding stepfamilies makes it difficult for everyone to understand how to behave. It's therefore up to you and your partner to decide how you want things to work – and make sure you let everyone know what's important to you. So if it makes you feel sad when your brother doesn't buy your stepchild a present, or your siblings don't include your stepchildren in family get-togethers, try and find a way of letting them know how you would like them to behave in future, without causing a family war!

YOUR PARENTS

One of the key relationships we tend to rely on throughout our life is that with our parents. When we need help or reassurance it's often our parents that we turn to for support as a 'constant' in our lives. So when we make a life-changing decision to move in with a new partner who also has children it's natural for them to be wary and want to protect us. For stepmums who also have their own children, parents will no doubt worry about the effect on their grandchildren, whether they will get on with your partner and be happy in the new family. While most parents want to support their children, it's common for them to struggle to come to terms with your new family in the early days of a relationship.

> *Rachel had been living with her partner Barry for two years. She had two young children from her previous marriage who now lived for the majority of the time with Rachel and Barry, and Barry had a young son from his previous marriage who came to stay with them regularly. Rachel had divorced her first husband a year before moving in with Barry. She had found it an extremely difficult and emotional time and really needed the support of her parents during the turmoil. But now her life had turned a corner. She was very happy with Barry and the children but frustratingly her relationship with her parents had become really*

distant. Whenever they went to visit her parents she felt that they didn't welcome Barry as they had her first husband. Wherever they went in the house there were photos of Rachel's first wedding, or Rachel and her first husband. They were constantly referring to times when Rachel was with her first husband and Rachel found herself always trying to change the subject. She felt really embarrassed for Barry and wished they could try and look forward rather than back.

Divorce or separation is considered to be the second most stressful life event you can experience, whether or not you are the partner who left, with only death seen as more traumatic. However, when a person dies, the grieving process is accepted and recognised by everyone equally. First there is disbelief, followed by anger and pain, and eventually acceptance, when everyone can finally move on. When the death is that of a relationship rather than an individual, there's still a grieving process to go through but it's often accompanied by feelings of guilt and failure, which get in the way of the healing process. Getting over a relationship can take a long time, regardless of whether you initiated the split or not.

In Rachel's case, she was only on her own for a year after the breakdown of her first marriage before settling down with Barry. Although she had come to terms with the end of her relationship – the last two years had been difficult between them although they'd tried to work things through – it was obvious that her parents were still grieving for their loss. They hadn't been able to let go of the idea of the idyllic family that they thought their daughter had been part of and had now somehow lost.

When I spoke to Rachel I helped her realise that her parents weren't trying to make things difficult for Barry, but were just trying to adjust to the changes at their own pace. I discovered that Rachel had not talked to them about the problems in her first marriage so the end of the relationship came as a bolt out of the blue. I encouraged Rachel to try and talk to her parents and help them understand that she was starting again and while they all had their memories of happier times, she wanted their help in building a new life with Barry without the constant reminders of her 'old' life. The changes were gradual but slowly her parents began to accept Rachel's new relationship with Barry. After holidays or family celebrations, Rachel made sure that she sent her parents new photographs of her family. And over time, they built up happy memories of their own that they could share and talk about whenever they met up.

It's vital that you give your parents – and other family members – time to adjust to the changes in your family. The decision to move in with your partner was something the two of you discussed together. It's likely that your parents weren't part of that decision and now they need time to get to know your new partner and his children. Often this is done in parallel with grieving over previous losses, so it's important not to rush anyone. Help them understand the new rules, how you'd like them to treat your new family and over time you'll get there.

YOUR IN-LAWS

In addition to maintaining your relationships with your direct family members, joining a stepfamily also means learning to manage your relationships with your new in-laws. Stepmothers often get less support from their in-laws than women in first families, which is usually related to the in-laws' ongoing relationship with their grandchildren's biological mother. Often in-laws feel torn between maintaining a relationship with the former partner and building a relationship with the new one. Their support is frequently given to the former partner in an effort to keep close links with their grandchildren and offer practical support with childcare.

As a stepmother you're following in someone else's footsteps and the fact that there are children from that relationship means that your partner's ex will always be a part of your life with your partner – and, to an extent, his extended family's life. Your partner's ex may still visit his parents with the children or perhaps she gets on well with your partner's siblings and their children. This can create difficult and complex relationships, with no one quite sure what the etiquette is.

One stepmother, Nicola, who had been in a relationship with her partner for almost 10 years, was still struggling to understand her relationship with her in-laws and even after all these years felt like an outsider.

Nicola had a young daughter when she first met her partner Steve and he had a young son. Steve's parents found it hard to come to terms with his divorce and worried that this would mean they would lose touch with their grandson, whom they adored. They also made it clear to Steve that they wanted to see their grandson on his own without Nicola's daughter. Nicola and Steve found this very hard and felt it was pulling apart the family they were trying to bring together so they persevered for the first two years of their relationship, making regular family trips with both children. But over time their relationship with Steve's parents became more strained as they were clearly finding it very difficult to adapt to the new family arrangements. Steve's parents started to see more of their grandson through visiting Steve's ex-wife. Cards and presents for birthdays and Christmases stopped arriving for Steve's son as they began sending them via Steve's ex. Nicola and Steve were left feeling confused and frustrated. Although they still see Steve's parents the relationship is quite remote. After so many years, they have come to accept the situation but often wonder how they could have changed the outcome.

It's vital that you and your partner set the rules for your family. Setting these rules can be difficult as everyone tiptoes around issues, not wanting to rock the boat and cause even more heartache. But it is something you can achieve as it's within your control, within your own family unit. However, trying to set rules in the wider realm of parents, brothers, sisters, aunts and uncles is nigh on impossible. Nicola and Steve couldn't force his parents not to see their grandson with his ex-wife and not to send his presents there but they could try and make them understand how their actions affected them. From talking to Nicola and Steve it became clear that Steve's parents needed more time to come to terms with the changes. Their main concern was for their grandson. As they lived a long way away, and Steve only saw his son for weekends and holidays, they were worried that this would mean even less contact for them. The reality was probably that their contact wouldn't have changed in terms of the frequency – but of course they also had to accept that their new daughter-in-law had a child of her own. They just needed more time to adjust. Although Steve and Nicola initially rejected their request to only see their grandson it might have been easier to start off this way and gradually introduce Nicola's daughter. Their main concern was in losing touch with their grandson so they secured this by keeping in touch with their ex-daughter-in-law – at the expense of their relationship with their son and his partner.

If you find that your in-laws keep in touch with your partner's ex, try and understand the reasons. Is it simply because they're worried about losing touch with their grandchildren (as in Nicola and Steve's case) or is it because they have a close relationship with his ex and want to continue seeing them? If it's the former try and reassure them that they are welcome as part of your family to see their grandchildren. Try and balance visits so that they see their grandchildren on their own as well as with the rest of the family. Above all, build new memories together and new traditions so that they aren't forever stuck in the past. If, however, your in-laws just get on well with your partner's ex then that is something you will have to accept. The relationship is not exclusive – just because they see her doesn't mean they can't see you. Giving people ultimatums – such as 'it's her or me' – often backfires. Take the moral high ground.

Worry about the things you can affect rather than things that are out of your control. If it's important to you that you have a good relationship with your in-laws then talk to your partner and work out what could be stopping you.

YOUR RELATIONSHIP WITH FRIENDS

Our friends are a very important part of our support network. We need them to bolster the support we get from our partner and family members as they offer support that is often one step removed from emotion. If we're angry with our partner it's sometimes easier to talk things through with a friend who can help us put some perspective into the situation before we lose the plot completely. We can share our knowledge and experience with our friends, whether it's advice on taming a toddler, dealing with an unruly teenager or simply using them as a sounding board for when we're feeling down. Friends are also a vital part of our support mechanism when we can't rely on the support of our partner or other family members. However, some research has suggested that stepmums have less support from friends than biological mums. If we take this statistic with the fact that stepmums often receive less support from their in-laws, you begin to paint a picture of a potentially poor support network for stepmums who are trying to perform a difficult job under pressure. If they aren't getting the support they need from those around them they are more likely to feel stressed and anxious, and struggle to continue their role in the stepfamily.

But why is it that stepmothers should have less support

from their friends? Well, often becoming part of a stepfamily can bring a number of changes in women's circumstances. For example they may choose to move to a different area to be with their new partner. This may be too far away from their friends to maintain a close relationship. Similarly, they may have to change jobs, either due to the location or even perhaps to take on a more full-time role in caring for their stepchildren. Their new commitments in the stepfamily may mean less free time to spend with friends as they try to build their new family home together, or even engender a feeling that they no longer have much in common with their single friends.

Although becoming part of a stepfamily can have an effect on our friendships, it depends on the type of step-mother you are. So, for example, if you already have children of your own, it's likely that your circle of friends will include busy mums who can share in your stories of your children and now your stepchildren. However, if you don't have children of your own, you're more likely to have single friends who are more used to partying with you than sharing babysitting duties! And if you take on the role of stepmum full-time, this can have a far bigger impact on your social life than a part-time role, with less free time to find to devote to catching up with friends without the children being around.

It can be a lonely job being a stepmother, feeling no one understands your role or the problems it can cause. As one stepmother commented:

I didn't have children when I became a step-parent and none of my friends had children so they didn't understand the commitment of being a step-parent.

They just expected me to be the same as before but I wasn't. I had a new partner and a ready-made family that I needed to consider. Eventually they just stopped asking me to join them when they were going out.

EMILY, STEPMUM FOR TWO YEARS TO TWO STEPCHILDREN
AGED SEVEN AND FOUR

Another stepmum felt that although she hadn't lost any of her friends, their relationship had changed significantly. As she commented:

Many of my friends don't understand stepfamilies. I didn't have any friends who were step-parents, so there was no one who could understand you and so you have this gap. I haven't really lost friends, just the closeness. I feel I can't really talk to them about any of the problems I have. We can talk on a superficial level but that's not what I really need.

SOPHIE, STEPMUM FOR THREE YEARS TO STEPDAUGHTER
AGED FIVE

HOW TO WIDEN YOUR SUPPORT NETWORK

The crucial thing is to recognise the importance of our friends to our overall well-being. If you think that your support network is looking a little sparse, try and take steps to turn things round. If you've lost touch with friends simply because of demands from your new family, make the effort to rebuild those friendships. Whether it's one day every week, or one evening every month, make sure that you make time for your friends. If you feel that they don't understand the things you have to deal with take the time to help them understand! A good friend will want to help – even if they're unfamiliar with the type of problems you have, they can still be there for you. It might actually help that they are more removed from the problem. Or if you've had to move away from your friends when you moved in with your partner, try and find ways of making new friends. Get to know your neighbours, join a local gym, take up a new sport. Anything to make yourself feel part of the community, and to build relationships with people outside your immediate family. And just because you've moved doesn't mean you have to lose touch with old friends. Invite them to visit for the day or the weekend. Make them feel welcome in your new family and help them get to know your partner and stepchildren.

Hopefully you now understand how important it is to surround yourself with people who you can turn to for help and advice. Individuals who have a strong social network benefit from better overall well-being. They are more likely to cope better when stressful situations present themselves and are less likely to suffer from symptoms of depression and anxiety. While family, friends and, of course, our partner are the main support mechanisms we turn to, these can be supplemented by other, more targeted, support groups. As I discovered myself, being a stepmother can be a very isolating experience. You can feel that no one understands what you're going through or can provide any answers. It's tempting to stop talking about your difficulties and just hope it will all blow over. The problem with this is that the issues won't go away and over time you'll just feel worse.

WHO'S IN YOUR SUPPORT NETWORK?

Take some time to think about the people you rely on. Think about the three areas of practical help, emotional support and just going out and enjoying yourself.

> ➤ I can get practical help from...
> ➤ I can get emotional support from...
> ➤ I have fun with...

Who do you turn to? Work out where the weaknesses are and try and put together a plan of action. Enlist the help of your partner to put in place the support you both need. In a perfect world we expect to be able to turn to our families, our friends or our partner to help make sense of our problems and guide us when we're feeling a bit unsure of ourselves. Unfortunately, we don't live in a perfect world and we all have to make the best of what we have. Learn to accept that there will be things you can't fix. Maybe your in-laws are still grieving over the end of their son's marriage and can't accept you in their lives for the time being; or your friends are more interested in going out clubbing than a night in babysitting with a bottle of wine and a DVD. Try and 'educate' your family and friends on the differences between first families and stepfamilies and help them understand how they could help you cope better.

If after reading this chapter you feel that you don't have the support you need from your family and friends, start to look for other support mechanisms. While there are very few support groups specifically for stepfamilies, you could always consider joining a parenting group. It's a good way to meet other families and parents and there may well be others there who are part of a stepfamily. These kinds of community support groups can be very effective at increasing self-esteem, well-being and confidence in parenting abilities. Don't be afraid to tell people you are a stepmum either. While it may feel easier to merge in with everyone else and let them assume you're a biological mum, if you try and hide, it can make it harder for other stepmums to find you!

Whether you're part of a stepfamily or not, everyone needs support, but with all the added complications of step-family life it helps to have as much support as you can muster!

Dealing with Resentment
and Ambiguity

It's very common for stepmothers at times to feel angry and resentful of their role in the stepfamily. Here is how one stepmother described her feelings when asked how she felt about her role as a stepmother.

> *Being a stepmother is so much harder than I imagined. When I first started seeing my stepchildren it was fine. But then all of a sudden, every other weekend we have to have his children. I can't explain how hard I find it to cope. It's often the small things that begin to irritate. I really resent them when on a Friday night I hear them coming across the path and I go into such a foul mood. They come in and they give me a kiss and I try very hard to be happy. But it is just so hard. I thought it would be easier once I'd had my own baby but I find myself using her as an excuse to escape, taking her out for a walk as soon as they arrive.*
>
> JENNY, STEPMUM FOR FIVE YEARS TO TWO CHILDREN
> AGED ELEVEN AND NINE

Many stepmums struggle with feelings of resentment towards their stepchildren and Jenny's experiences are far from unique. Like Jenny, they struggle to move on and accept their new family commitments. Often, many stepmums feel jealous of the time their stepchildren spend with their partner and themselves. Then there is the fact that most describe their role as confusing or ambiguous, not knowing how to define their role in the family. While they feel that they take on some parenting responsibilities there are limitations to their roles, which inevitably leads to ambiguity and frustration.

It is essential that you, and your partner, work out what role you should take as a stepmum: perhaps you're more comfortable with a hands-on approach, or maybe a more remote relationship with your stepchildren is appropriate for the time being. If you know what part you are to play in your stepchildren's lives, you are less likely to feel confused and resentful. Not being sure of your stepmum role means that you are likely to feel frustrated and not in control, which can lead to anxiety and 'catastrophic' thinking, thereby establishing a set of feelings that feed off each other and can turn into a vicious circle of ambiguity, resentment and anxiety.

RECOGNISING RESENTMENT

I have strong values and I believe children need to understand what's right and wrong. My stepdaughter needs telling she's wrong sometimes but I can't be the one because I'm not her parent. Neither of her parents discipline her and I get really frustrated with her behaviour… We used to be really close, she used to call me her second mum, but we've drifted apart

*because I don't like the person she's become any more.
It's a real shame because I don't think she gets a great
deal of parenting at home as her mum treats her like
her best friend.*

CARLA, STEPMUM FOR 10 YEARS TO STEPDAUGHTER AGED 15

It's often the case that stepmothers desperately want to help
raise their stepchildren but are left on the sidelines to watch
others instil their own rules and discipline. In many cases,
they simply stop trying and as Carla explained, their relationship becomes more and more distant over time.

So the important thing here is to recognise that although
these feelings are common among stepmothers, there are
things we can do to minimise them and improve the overall
outlook for our families. There are no instant fixes, but with
time and patience you can learn to be more positive.

First, you need to understand whether these areas are
particular issues for you in your family. The following questionnaire will measure your levels of resentment and ambiguity.

Gauge your resentment

Take a few minutes to respond to the following statements
about how you feel about your stepfamily. Please try to be as
honest as you can.

1. None of my family or friends understands the
   difficulties stepfamilies have.

Strongly disagree	*1*
Disagree	*2*

Neither agree nor disagree	*3*
Agree	*4*
Strongly agree	*5*

2. I don't look forward to my stepchildren's visits.

Strongly disagree	*1*
Disagree	*2*
Neither agree nor disagree	*3*
Agree	*4*
Strongly agree	*5*

3. I resent taking on the additional household burden associated with my stepchildren.

Strongly disagree	*1*
Disagree	*2*
Neither agree nor disagree	*3*
Agree	*4*
Strongly agree	*5*

4. I feel sad when I think how different my life would be if we weren't a stepfamily.

Strongly disagree	*1*
Disagree	*2*
Neither agree nor disagree	*3*
Agree	*4*
Strongly agree	*5*

5. I try and avoid telling people I'm a stepmother.

Strongly disagree	*1*
Disagree	*2*
Neither agree nor disagree	*3*

Agree	*4*
Strongly agree	*5*

6. I'm often confused as to how much or when to parent
   my stepchild.

Strongly disagree	*1*
Disagree	*2*
Neither agree nor disagree	*3*
Agree	*4*
Strongly agree	*5*

7. I sometimes hesitate in my interactions for fear they
   think I'm the wicked stepmother.

Strongly disagree	*1*
Disagree	*2*
Neither agree nor disagree	*3*
Agree	*4*
Strongly agree	*5*

8. I feel inadequate as a stepmother.

Strongly disagree	*1*
Disagree	*2*
Neither agree nor disagree	*3*
Agree	*4*
Strongly agree	*5*

9. I sometimes fear I'm the wicked stepmother of the
   Cinderella story.

Strongly disagree	*1*
Disagree	*2*
Neither agree nor disagree	*3*

Agree	4
Strongly agree	5

10. I often wonder if I'm being a good step-parent.

Strongly disagree	1
Disagree	2
Neither agree nor disagree	3
Agree	4
Strongly agree	5

Add up your scores for statements 1 to 5. You should have a total of between 5 and 25. This is your resentment score. A higher score reflects greater feelings of resentment towards your role in your stepfamily.

Score

5–10 You have very little resentment towards your role.

11–15 You have some feelings of resentment but these are generally much lower than others in your position may feel.

16–20 You have quite high resentment which you need to keep in check. Use the tips in this chapter to help you understand your feelings and how to reduce your resentment.

Above 20 Your score reflects very strong feelings of resentment towards your role. Use this chapter to develop a strategy for moving forward with the help of your partner.

Now add up your scores for statements 6 to 10. Again, your total score should be between 5 and 25. This forms your ambiguity score. A higher score in this area is an indication of greater confusion and uncertainty about your role.

Score

5–10   Well done! You have managed to define your role within your family and have laid out clear boundaries.

11–16   You have some feelings of confusion or ambiguity about your role in the family but these are generally lower than average.

17–20   Your score suggests that you may be struggling to define your role in the family and as a consequence you are confused about your position.

Above 20 Your score suggests that you are finding it very difficult to deal with your role as a stepmother. Use this section of the book to help you develop strategies, ideally with your partner, to clearly define your role.

UNDERSTANDING THE CAUSES OF RESENTMENT

The resentment score effectively measures the difficulty a stepmother finds in accepting her role within the family. This resentment can manifest itself both practically and emotionally. It may be dealing with the additional strain of having the responsibility of looking after more people in the family that tips you over the edge or you may simply find it more difficult to accept that your family is not a traditional nuclear family. Either way, you can start to resent your stepchildren and treat them as the cause of the problem.

It's been found that stepmothers who don't have biological children of their own are more likely to feel resentful than stepmothers who have brought their own children into the stepfamily. Type B stepmothers (residential stepchildren and no biological children of their own from previous relationships, see page 18) tend to feel more resentful from a practical level, having full-time responsibility for their stepchildren. Many also feel isolated from their family and friends who aren't able to understand the new commitments that they have taken on board when they became part of a stepfamily. As these stepmothers didn't have children of their own prior to this relationship, the change in their lifestyle is even starker for them. Conversely, for Type C stepmothers (see page 20), the changes are less extreme. With children of their own prior to the relationship, they are more used to the demands on their time as a mother. They are also more likely to have a circle of friends who are also parents and thus more able to understand the changes to their lifestyle.

COSTS AND REWARDS

Understanding the way resentment can build is extremely important, because you need to spot the signs and work out how you can make it reduce or even disappear. The best way to explain this is by using Social Exchange Theory. This theory looks at the 'costs' and 'benefits' of being involved in a relationship and suggests that these need to be in balance for individuals to feel happy and content. How we feel about a relationship with another person depends on our perceptions of 'fairness' within the relationship, balancing what we put into a relationship with what we get out of it. The theory suggests that when the rewards exceed the costs, people are more likely to be committed to these relationships and to maintain them; however, if the costs exceed the rewards people are more likely to consider leaving the relationship. Let's look at a couple of examples to illustrate how this might work.

Scenario 1

Prior to meeting your partner, you were a single girl with your own apartment in the centre of town, had a great circle of friends and enjoyed going out every weekend. You subsequently move in with your partner and his two young children to his house out of town. As the children are only small it's difficult to go out with your partner often. Instead you tend to stay in more or maybe invite friends over – they tend to be more 'his' friends though, as yours are still young, free and single, and happier partying.

The 'costs' of your relationship, such as your loss of independence and social life, need to be balanced (in your head) by the rewards – such as your love for your partner, companionship or stability. But remember, the 'costs' and 'rewards' are purely subjective – what one individual sees as a cost may be a reward to another.

Scenario 2

Prior to meeting your partner you were living on your own with your two young children. Social life was a thing of the past – with no spare time, inclination or money! Although you loved being with your children you craved adult company.

With fewer major changes in your lifestyle, the 'costs' here might be related to balancing your time between your children and your stepchildren, or learning to set and uphold household rules for all the children. The 'rewards' in this scenario might be in finding emotional support from your partner and financial security.

While we generally don't make conscious decisions on labelling things in a relationship as 'costs' or 'rewards', there are times when all of us have felt things were 'unbalanced' or that we're doing more than our fair share. If you don't find a way to resolve this imbalance, the chances are you'll find yourself resenting the situation. But while this theory helps us understand why people might develop resentment or even anger, measuring these so-called 'costs and rewards' of a relationship is purely subjective. What one person sees as a 'cost' may actually be a reward to another and vice versa. However, despite these difficulties it can help you understand the things you value in a relationship.

Measuring costs and rewards

Spend a few minutes thinking about your own relationship in terms of the costs and rewards. This will help you under-stand how you categorise things, and what you might consider a cost in your relationship and what might be a reward. As always, there are no rights and wrongs to this exercise, Make sure you put the same amount of effort into considering both categories and include items that you would like to happen that perhaps don't currently (such as being cooked a meal by your partner, a cuddle from your stepson or a night out occasionally!) And remember to consider both practical and emotional items. The only rule is that for every cost item you must include a reward.

Costs	Rewards
(Include all the things that you see as a cost. This should include practical items, such as doing the laundry or taking the children to school, as well as emotional 'costs', such as feeling anxious about your stepchildren's visits, coping with the ex-wife or sharing your partner with his children.)	(Include all the things you enjoy in your stepfamily. Remember to include the small things, such as your partner telling you he loves you every day or a hug from your stepchild, as well as more tangible things, such as financial security or a family home.)
1.	
2.	
3.	
4.	
5.	
6.	
7.	
8.	
9.	
10.	

If you found this exercise hard and your costs are out-weighing your rewards, then we need to spend some time in trying to restore the balance in your relationship. Put simply, you can do one of three things:

➤ reduce the costs
➤ increase the rewards
➤ change your perception of what is a cost or a reward

1. Reducing the costs in your relationship

It's likely that your list included both physical costs, such as cooking and cleaning for the family, and emotional costs, such as having to 'share' your partner with his children. Try and separate these because we can deal with them differently. It's almost certain that in becoming a stepmother you took on board more household tasks. Whether it's washing sports kit or simply feeding extra mouths, the chances are you will have taken on some of these roles. The question to ask yourself is whether you think this is a fair split between you and your partner and the rest of the family members. If these tasks get you down and are causing you to resent your situation then you need to find ways of reducing them. It may be that you could ask your partner or stepchildren/children to help more, or perhaps if time's the problem but finances would stretch, you could afford a cleaner to take some of the strain.

In terms of emotional costs, you need to focus not on the cost as such, but on how you can reduce the perceived cost. For example, if you're finding it hard to come to terms with the changes of being part of a stepfamily, you need to learn to somehow *accept* these changes – but also learn to associate these 'costs' with benefits. So if you're finding it hard to be positive about your stepchildren's visit and only associate it with negatives, such as a loss of privacy or physical space, try and link the visits with positive thoughts. Perhaps your partner could cook a meal for the two of you when the children have gone to bed, or you could share a bottle of wine and watch a good film. Arrange an event that you can all enjoy, or agree to spend some time together as a family, but compromise with time out for you with your friends for a couple of hours.

How you cope with a problem is linked to the amount of resentment you feel. So, if you can learn to adopt a more positive attitude and look for the benefit – rather than focusing on the negative aspect – you're likely to reduce your anxiety and feelings of resentment. If, for example, you've started to resent your stepchildren's visits, rather than focusing on your own emotions and feelings, try and think about how your partner is feeling. The visit may not benefit you significantly but your partner may have been looking forward to seeing his children all week. Or if you and your partner have had an argument related to your stepchildren and you find yourself somehow 'blaming' them for the situation, try and use the experience to learn from. How could you and your partner have dealt with things differently that might not have led to the argument? How can you improve things in the longer term? Once we start focusing on the negative aspects of anything, whether it's parenting or anything else in life, we look for things that support our view that it is difficult or problematic. If you can shift your view, even slightly, to focus on the positives you're likely to find things looking a whole lot brighter.

Understanding your thought patterns

Try and do this exercise with a friend. Cast your mind back over the past couple of weeks to work out when you argued with your partner. Perhaps it was over your stepchildren's behaviour, or the way your partner dealt with his ex. Whatever the issue, work out what you *thought* about the situation. Did you blame your partner, your stepchildren? Then tell your friend or write down how you *felt* at the time. Were you angry with your partner? Did you feel resentful or anxious? Finally, what did you *do* to address the problem? Did you confront your partner? Or did you just bottle up your feelings?

Now ask your friend to challenge these thoughts. Were you being fair? Could there have been an alternative explanation? Could you change the way you approached the problem? By focusing on negative thoughts it's possible to change the way you feel and ultimately improve the outcome. Use this exercise to start to understand negative thought patterns. In this way you should start to see a change in the way you approach a problem, focusing more on being constructive than destructive.

It's also important that you try and get support from your family – particularly your in-laws, as this will help you feel less resentful. If your in-laws have remained close to your partner's ex, perhaps you feel it's difficult to build a relationship with them, or perhaps they haven't made an effort to welcome you into their family. Whatever the case, it's important to understand that support from your in-laws can help you feel part of your new family and help lower any resentment you feel.

2. Increasing the rewards in your relationship

So this is the good bit. You will already have identified lots of good things that happen in your relationship – the kind of things that brought you together as a couple in the first place. Now's the time to revisit this. We all lead busy lives and it's inevitable that over time we become complacent and forget the small things that can make a difference. As discussed in Chapter 2, it's vital to concentrate on your partnership as it's the one thing that holds up the rest of your family. Look at your list and identify the things that make you happy, that you appreciate in your partner and the children. The first thing to do is make sure that they know that these are the things which make the difference. Often we assume that if something makes us happy it must be the same for everyone else. Charlotte, who has been a stepmum for nine years, told me how she had managed to increase the 'rewards' in her relationship with her stepson who was now 11. Like most mums, Charlotte treasured cuddles from her children and when she became a stepmum she just assumed that she would get cuddles from her stepson. But over time she realised that that wasn't what he was used to. Although he clearly had a loving relationship with his mum, they weren't big on cuddles. But over the years he's learned that Charlotte really values cuddles and he makes a special effort just for her. It makes her feel great when her stepson spontaneously gives her a cuddle because she knows he's doing it just for her. It's made their relationship special – and different from the one he has with his mum. Unless she'd told him how she felt Charlotte would never have got her cuddles – not because her stepson didn't love her, because he didn't value them the same way she did.

So work out what's important to you – what you enjoy and value – and make sure you let your loved ones know. That way, you'll encourage them to do more of the things that make you happy. And don't forget to encourage your stepchildren to let you know what makes them happy too – don't assume you know. They might surprise you!

3. Change your perception of what is a cost and what is a reward

As I said earlier, the notion of costs and rewards in a relationship is subjective. It's only *your* view of what constitutes a cost or a reward. While you may have equal numbers of costs and rewards on your list they are probably not equal in value. For example, the fact that you have to make the children's beds in the morning or make the packed lunches for school can't really equate to your partner telling you he loves you, can it? Sometimes we become overly irritated by the small things in life. And because we don't tell anyone how we feel they can become unreasonably important in our minds and overshadow the things that really matter. Take some time to look at your list and try and get a balanced perspective.

DEALING WITH ANGER

Often the resentment that stepmothers feel is hidden from their partners and family. When I spoke to Jenny, for example, while she was happy to tell me in confidence how she felt about her stepchildren's visit, she had not shared these views with her partner, partly because she knew how this would hurt him, but partly because she was ashamed to have those feelings. Instead she attempted to reconcile her feelings by limiting contact with her stepchildren and pushing the thoughts to the back of her mind. However, sometimes this resentment can rear its head in the form of anger, where violent arguments seem to blow out of nowhere. Sometimes, we realise that our response was out of proportion to the offence but we often feel powerless to understand or stop ourselves. As Emma told me:

> *I really dread the weekends when Dave's children come over to visit. I start feeling anxious days before their visit. It seems like every time they come, me and Dave end up arguing with each other. They're not really naughty children but they just seem to do things deliberately to annoy me. When I tell them off Dave doesn't support me or just seems to make excuses for them which makes me even more cross. It's like they've won again. I just don't know what to do any more.*
>
> EMMA, STEPMUM FOR TWO YEARS TO TWO STEPCHILDREN
> AGED SIX AND EIGHT

Emma had found herself caught in a negative spiral. She expected to have a bad time when her stepchildren came to visit and looked for any behaviour from them that reinforced her view. She became angry and frustrated when this happened which only left her feeling more resentful of their next visit.

If you can identify with Emma you need to analyse what's actually making you react the way you do and is your reaction reasonable and fair?

➤ What makes you angry?
➤ Why do you get so angry?
➤ When does it happen?

Think about these questions and the times you get angry. Ask yourself what it is that actually makes you feel angry. In Emma's case, the answer here was simply her stepchildren made her angry and her anger resulted from her underlying resentment. She felt that she couldn't rely on the support of her partner, who always seemed to 'side' with his children. Clearly there were probably times when Emma's anger at her stepchildren may have been justified. They may have mis-behaved and deserved to be told off but Emma's behaviour had probably made it hard for her partner to recognise when her anger was justified.

What Emma needed to do was to understand what triggered her anger. Clearly she needed to accept that the children would be coming to stay and to try and be more positive about the visits and to not assume that a row would be inevitable. What was it that her stepchildren did that seemed to make her angry? When I spoke to Emma she told me that during the weekends her stepchildren's mum would phone them to check they were okay. She couldn't hear the conversations but she could hear the way they spoke to their mother and told her they loved her. She realised that they spoke to her without the same affection. She found herself then looking for some show of affection or thanks from them, which inevitably she didn't get. So if she cooked a meal and they forgot to say 'thank you' she would tell them how ungrateful they were which then started off the inevitable row.

When Emma realised that the real trigger was the phone calls she spent some time explaining the way she felt to her partner. Once he understood he arranged for his children to talk to their mother when they were out of the house so Emma didn't hear them. He also agreed to support Emma more when it was necessary to tell the children off and they also developed some simple house rules which they could all sign up to. Over time, Emma found that the arguments became less and less and she no longer dreaded the weekends. Once she realised the real reason for her anger she found she could cope with the feelings she had and they became far less destructive.

Anger triggers

If you think that you need to find a way of dealing with your anger, take some time to think about the triggers for your arguments.

Make sure you get to the root of the problem. Try and understand what triggers your anger. Perhaps you get angry when your stepchildren are visiting because you don't feel supported by your partner, or maybe you find it hard to come to terms with being a stepfamily, or your anger may be related to financial issues such as the maintenance your partner pays to his ex. Whatever the issue, make sure you're honest with yourself and identify the true cause of your feelings.

UNDERSTANDING ROLE AMBIGUITY

I was really looking forward to Anna's play. I had been practising the songs with her for weeks and had helped make her costume. I went to the school to get tickets and was told I couldn't have one as tickets were limited to two per family and as both her mother and father wanted to go we couldn't have a third ticket. I was really upset and felt worthless. I had put so much effort into helping Anna and couldn't even see her perform.

PAULA, STEPMUM FOR FOUR YEARS TO STEPDAUGHTER AGED SEVEN

Role ambiguity is an issue which all stepmothers face at some point. While many of you would empathise with Paula, an equal number of you may feel she was wrong to have had such high expectations and shouldn't have become so involved in her stepdaughter's play. This highlights one of the main issues with being a stepmother. There are no rules. There are no social norms or endorsement of step-parenting as there are with biological parenting. Imagine the same scenario where only the mother was allowed to attend the school play and not the father. There would be outrage – and rightly so. But leave out step-parents and no one really cares.

Psychologists have for many years believed that the stress experienced by stepmothers was in part caused by the absence of so-called 'social norms' or role models to help them define their role within their stepfamily. As the roles are so vague, it's difficult for stepmothers to assess whether they are succeeding (or failing) in their roles, leading to ever-increasing confusion and anxiety. This issue of role ambiguity is well recognised within stepfamilies, suggesting that the stepmother often lacks a role model and whatever expectations she does have of herself tend to be unrealistic. As a consequence some stepmothers feel frustrated in trying to fill a largely undefined role for which they have no training.

Given that there are no prescribed roles for stepmothers it's therefore left up to individuals to carve out their own role in the stepfamily. Some happily take on board a strong parental role, becoming a 'second mother' to their step-children. They set and impose household rules for their stepchildren, they discipline them, care for them when their partners are absent, are included in school activities and major milestones such as weddings and graduations. Others are happy to take more of a back seat. They support their partners but are less involved in their stepchildren's day-to-day activities.

There are many reasons for taking a different stance on your role within the stepfamily. For stepmothers who care for their stepchildren for the majority of the time, it makes sense for them to take on board a parental-like role, whereas for stepmothers who rarely see their stepchildren it's clearly harder to be more active in their stepchildren's lives.

However, neither approach is right or wrong and depends to a large extent on your individual family circumstances. Issues only arise when there is a discrepancy between family members on their idea of the role the stepmother should play. Stepmothers have to find their own way, work out what seems to work for them, their partner and their stepchildren. While Paula desperately wanted to watch her stepdaughter perform in her school play, she realised that as far as the school rules were concerned, her attendance was secondary to the parents, regardless of her involvement and support to her stepdaughter.

Paula's experiences are far from unique, unfortunately. While schools are becoming more aware of stepfamilies and their needs, there are no recognised rules for extended family members. Another stepmother spoke of her sadness at not being included in her stepson's recent graduation. She had a close relationship with her stepson but respected his desire not to upset his mother by inviting his stepmother to this important event.

Stepmothers who are happiest in their roles have generally found a common ground on which to stake their role in the family. While some may be sad that they can't play a fuller role in their stepchildren's lives, they are nevertheless content to live by the status quo, recognising that it is more important to discuss issues and expectations of their role with their partner and reach consensus than continually wish for something that's unattainable.

If you find that you're confused about your role in your family, take some time to talk to your partner about his expectations and your own. If the differences are important to either of you then it's equally important to discuss them and try and find a compromise. But remember that there is a balance to everything. It's no good making *you* happy if it means your stepchildren are in pieces, and equally it's not acceptable to give in to your partner or stepchildren at the expense of your feelings. So, for example, if it's important to you that you attend your stepchildren's school play or parents' evening, talk to your partner about it. Discuss the reasons you haven't been included. It might be that he simply didn't think you'd want to go. Alternatively, if there are reasons behind you not attending try and find a solution that works for everyone. Maybe the play is being shown twice and you could attend one performance with your partner and your stepchildren's mother could attend on the other day. Teachers are sympathetic to children's circumstances and are usually happy to talk to parents outside of parents' evenings, so it may be possible to meet your stepchildren's teacher and talk about their progress with your partner so that you feel included in any decisions concerning their education.

Conversely, if you don't want to attend these types of event but your partner thinks you should, be open to understanding why it's important for him and help him understand why you don't want to be included. Try and find a compromise that suits you both and that your stepchildren are happy with.

It is up to stepmothers to define their role and make it work for themselves and their families. The most important consideration is to jointly agree on the scope of the role and stick to it. Keep talking to your partner and find out what works for you. What works for you and your family might not work for another family. That doesn't matter. What matters is your well-being. If you're happy and content in your role and feel supported and loved by your partner, you will feel ready to take on the world.

STEPMOTHER PARENTING STYLE

Although there are no clear guidelines for the role of the stepmother, women tend to adopt one of five broad parenting styles. You should be able to find the style that closely resembles yours. Remember that there are positive and negative aspects to each style.

The third parent

Many women believe that step- and biological parenting are pretty much identical and try to behave and feel exactly the same towards their stepchildren as they would their own children. They see this as logical and natural. By treating their stepchildren in this way, stepmums are less likely to experience any role ambiguity as they are clear about their role as a 'parent' to their stepchildren. This can make life easier for both the stepmum and the rest of the family. However, if the stepchildren don't accept their stepmother as a mother figure this can lead to conflict within the family, which in turn could lead to the stepmum feeling rejected and becoming resentful and angry at the situation. There could also be further conflict between the stepmother and her partner if he doesn't agree on her taking such an active role in parenting his children.

However, this can be a really positive role for a step-mother to adopt, as long as everyone in the family unit is in agreement. If you feel that you view yourself as an 'extra' parent then it's important that your stepchildren understand that you're not trying to 'replace' their mother. Women who have been successful in adopting this approach have generally tried to build some form of relationship with their stepchildren's biological mother, to enable them to share information and make the transition between homes easier for everyone. As one stepmum said:

> There aren't any rules that say you can only have two parents. Why can't three be better than two? My stepdaughter has two 'mums'. We're both very different but we love her equally.
>
> JACKIE, STEPMUM FOR FIVE YEARS TO HER STEPDAUGHTER
> AGED EIGHT

The 'super stepmum'

These women go out of their way to be seen to be conscientious stepmothers to their stepchildren. Many adopt this style to try and dispel the myth of the wicked stepmother and typically shower their stepchildren with love, affection and material gifts. They often avoid telling their stepchildren off, leaving their partner to discipline the kids. They want to prove to themselves and their partner that they can do a good job and they want to 'win round' the children. This can be successful but it's important to realise you can't always be superwoman! The children need time to get to know you – the real you.

The danger with this approach is that your stepchildren can start to take advantage of you. Many women who adopt this style avoid setting boundaries or disciplining their stepchildren in an effort to be popular. But if this approach doesn't work, and the stepchildren fail to show their appreciation for their stepmother, it can lead the stepmum to feel resentment towards the children and even her partner.

The 'back-seat' stepmother

Women who identify with this style have minimal involvement with their stepchildren. They tend to leave things to their partners. For example, when their partner spends time with the children they make their excuses and go and visit friends instead. They don't dislike their stepchildren but they don't feel they have a bond with them either. As far as they're concerned, their partner's children are just that, and they take a back seat. They see themselves as supportive to their partner but want to give their partner time to spend with his children – alone.

This approach can work in some cases, particularly where the father doesn't see his children very frequently and wants to spend as much time as possible with them. It may be that this is the style that works for your family and you and your partner have agreed that this is the best approach. The difficulties, however, stem from when you and your partner haven't agreed on this approach but it has become the default position.

This style is usually adopted after stepmothers have failed to make one of the other styles work for them. For example, some women may start off trying to be the super stepmum. However, when their efforts aren't appreciated or they feel rejected they can feel alienated and develop a distance from their stepchildren in an effort to minimise their hurt.

If you see yourself as someone who has stepped back from becoming involved with your partner's children, ask yourself if this is really what you and your partner want in the long term. Although it can be successful, particularly if the children don't visit regularly or are older, it can lead to feelings of isolation. If you would like to take a more active role, takes things slowly. Perhaps you could join your partner and his children on an activity over a weekend but let them have some time together without you. You don't have to be joined at the hip but it's about making memories and getting to know one another, so that you're more comfortable in each other's company.

The 'unsure' stepmother

These stepmothers are unsure of their position or role in the family and need reassurance and help. It is usually a style adopted by women who have no parenting experience and feel overwhelmed by their new-found responsibilities. They are unsure how to 'parent' their stepchild and seek help from their partner in setting boundaries and rules. This style is more likely to increase anxiety for stepmothers and can make it harder for the women to develop close relationships with their stepchildren.

If you feel that this is you, think about why you're not feeling too sure of yourself. What would help you grow your confidence? Do you need more support from your partner? Could he tell you more often that you're doing a great job? Try and talk to your partner about your worries. Be as specific as you can so that he can understand and help.

The 'friend'

This style is adopted by women who don't want to be a mother figure to their stepchildren but do want to take care of them. They develop close relationships with their stepchildren but accept that they will never replace the biological parents in their affections. This style seems to be particularly effective when the stepchildren have a close relationship with their biological mother as there is less comparison between the roles. It also seems to engender greater openness and trust between the step-parent and stepchildren and has been shown to be the most common style adopted by stepmothers. However, it's worth pointing out that it's easier to adopt this style when your stepchildren are a little bit older – let's face it, it's hard to be a friend to a toddler. It's important to remember, though, that even as a friend you need to be clear on house rules. You're still the adult and it's still your home.

The important thing is to recognise the style you most closely identify with and work out whether you are happy with that role. While stepmothers broadly adopt one of these styles at the outset, they generally gravitate to one after having attempted other styles. So, over time, those women who are uncertain about their role develop more confidence. They develop closer relationships with their stepchildren and may begin to identify more closely with the friendship style. Conversely, those that try to adopt a close parenting style early on in the relationship may find that they need to step back and take things more slowly.

INCREASING YOUR OVERALL WELL-BEING

Role ambiguity and resentment are often linked closely with stepmothers' well-being, so when feelings of resentment are running high and women are confused about their role, they generally feel more anxious. It is also likely to have a negative effect on their relationship with their partner.

If you can learn to reduce your feelings of resentment and anger and better define your role, you are likely to feel less anxious and overall be happier in your family.

What is anxiety?

Symptoms of anxiety can include irritability, excessive worrying, difficulty concentrating, avoidance of situations, increased dependency and restlessness. While some anxiety is considered a good thing – even essential, with an important function in relation to survival – too much anxiety over a prolonged period is not considered healthy. Life events play a significant role in increasing anxiety, such as illness, moving house, death or divorce. Anxiety is then maintained by these anxious thoughts, where individuals 'catastrophise' and distort the possible outcomes and probability of these outcomes. This is exacerbated by a lack of self-confidence and a reduced belief in their ability to carry out the activities successfully.

There is a link between how confused you are about the role you play in your stepfamily, the resentment you feel and the anxiety that results, with each one feeding off the previous, and forming a vicious circle. You need to break this circle in order to start to move forwards. As each area is linked with the others, a change in one is likely to positively affect the others. So, for example, if you can work with your partner to clarify your role in the family you are likely to be less anxious and worry less about your relationship with your stepchildren. This will in turn reduce any resentment you might feel towards your partner or stepchildren.

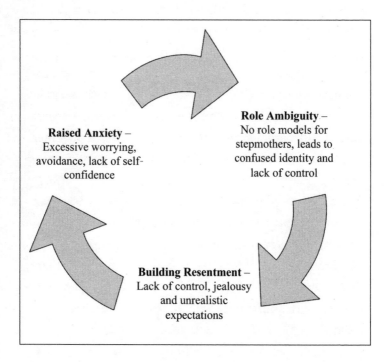

Role Ambiguity – No role models for stepmothers, leads to confused identity and lack of control

Raised Anxiety – Excessive worrying, avoidance, lack of self-confidence

Building Resentment – Lack of control, jealousy and unrealistic expectations

Start to work out what role you want to have in your new family and work with your partner and children to make it happen. Once you've reset your expectations you're on the right track. You can stop worrying and start building that confidence!

This chapter has looked at how resentment and ambiguity can affect you – and how one can feed off the other and draw you down into a spiral of discontentment and unhappiness. If you can learn to control these feelings by understanding the causes you're on your way to being a happier stepmum.

Resentment can stem from emotional or physical sources. You might feel taken for granted, like some sort of modern-day twist on Cinderella, where you're the one expected to cook and clean from dawn to dusk. Or perhaps you resent being left out of your partner's biological family, where no one consults you or includes you. However your resentment has grown, learn to identify why it has and think about the costs and rewards of your relationship. Once you've got everything balanced you'll start to feel less resentful and more optimistic about your future together.

As we've discussed, often the most difficult part of being a stepmum is working out what being a stepmum actually means to you. Think about the role you currently play in your family and try and map it to one of the most common types. There may not be a completely accurate match but you should be able to identify the closest one. As ever, there aren't any hard and fast rules: just make sure your partner understands (and agrees with!) the role you have in your family.

The Ex-factor

In a new relationship where there are no children from previous relationships, couples can effectively 'start again'. They have their memories – but that's all that really remains. While we know our partners have had other relationships we don't want to be – or need to be – reminded of them on a daily basis.

But that's exactly what step-parents *do* have to contend with. We have our partners, their children and even their ex-partners to cope with. They're all inextricably linked. Whether your stepchildren's mother plays a large or small part in their lives, or is completely absent, is largely irrelevant. They exist and can have a profound effect on the new relationships within the stepfamily. In fact, problems connected with their partner's ex are some of the most common issues stepmothers face.

UNDERSTANDING THE PROBLEM

The chance of a stepmother telling you how much they admire their stepchildren's mother or what a good mother they are is very unlikely. Instead you're more likely to hear them criticising them or their parenting abilities. So if you feel that the root of your problems lies with your partner's ex, you're far from alone!

Some of the most common types of questions asked by stepmothers are listed below – but you may well have others.

> ➤ Why do I feel excluded from my own family?
> ➤ Why do I care what she thinks?
> ➤ Why do I feel jealous of her?
> ➤ Why does she always seem to call the shots?
> ➤ Why can't she be a better mother to her children?
> ➤ Why do my in-laws favour her over me?
> ➤ Why does she expect my partner to support her financially?
> ➤ Why does she have to interfere with our lives?
> ➤ Why can't she stop phoning when her children are with us?

FEELING EXCLUDED FROM THE PREVIOUS FAMILY UNIT

Your partner has a very difficult job and needs to tread a fine line between balancing his 'new family' with his 'old'. He has to continually keep stepping into his 'old life' to maintain his relationship with his children before stepping back to the present. There will always be decisions to be made from which neither parent wants to be left out. When he steps back into his old life, his new partner can feel excluded.

Kathryn is a stepmother to her nine-year-old step-daughter. Recently her stepdaughter had been coughing a lot at night and seemed out of breath when they went on family bike rides. She thought her stepdaughter might be showing signs of asthma and suggested to her husband that he got her checked out.

But when she spoke to her husband he was quite dismissive and said he didn't think it was anything to worry about. That it would probably go away. As time went on Kathryn became really frustrated. The coughing was incessant and didn't seem to be getting better. She found herself wondering whether her stepdaughter was doing it on purpose to annoy her – before telling herself not to be so ridiculous! Eventually she persuaded her husband to take her seriously and he promised to talk to his ex about it. Months later, Kathryn's stepdaughter was finally diagnosed with asthma after her mum had taken her to the doctor's. Although Kathryn was relieved, she felt powerless. Even after the diagnosis, she constantly had to ask her husband what the doctor had said and what the treatment would be. She had been the first one to recognise the problem and yet she was the last one to be told anything!

Unfortunately, this is generally the experience of the stepparent, particularly if your stepchildren don't live with you all the time. Although Kathryn was trying to do her best for her stepdaughter, she didn't have the authority as a parent would to take control of her stepdaughter's illness. The responsibility here is on Kathryn's partner to keep her updated on her stepdaughter's progress and to thank her for being so concerned. It can feel frustrating not being able to take control. If it was your own child you would just take them to the doctor's immediately, without question. But imagine if it was the other way round. What if it was your child and their stepmother took them to the doctors? Obviously if it was an emergency that would be perfectly acceptable, but in the case of Kathryn and her step-daughter? It's possible that the biological mother might feel that it was up to her to make the decision. It's all about striking the right balance. As a stepmother you don't want to be excluded from decisions but sometimes you have to be on the sidelines.

If you feel you're being excluded from decisions or discussions between your partner and his ex, work out what it is you really want. Do you really want to be included more or is it simply the fear of being left out or ignored that hurts? Be honest with yourself and try and understand what you would like to change. Remember, you can still influence things – as in Kathryn's case. Try and be relaxed about your partner's relationship with his ex. Encourage him to be open with you about things he has to discuss with his ex so that he feels comfortable in talking about issues. This should help build trust between you and reduce any feelings you might have of feeling excluded. If you find yourself feeling jealous or envious about their ongoing relationship remind yourself of a few realities.

1. Your partner is being a responsible parent by maintaining a positive relationship with his ex.
2. Your partner's 'old life' will always be an important part of him because of his children – not because of his ex.
3. He has chosen to be with you – not his ex.
4. Jealousy can destroy a healthy relationship over time – don't let it.

5. Support your partner in his relationship with his ex – it will make you feel stronger and in control.

So remember, if you're feeling left out, put things into perspective. As a step-parent you are a step away from biological parenthood. That's not to say you can't be actively involved in your stepchildren's well-being, but your views will generally come second to their biological parents'.

WHY DO YOU CARE WHAT YOUR PARTNER'S EX THINKS OF YOU?

This is a real conundrum. Although the majority of stepmothers rarely meet their partner's ex – let alone go on to develop any form of relationship with her, they share a common desire in wanting their stepchildren to only say good things about them to their mothers! In a way, this is a reaction to the myth of the wicked stepmother. As one woman told me:

> *I don't know why but I'm always really anxious when it's time for my stepson to go back to his mum's. I want her to think I've looked after him well and that he's happy here. I always dread him saying that I told him off. I'd hate it if she mentioned it to my husband. I'd feel really bad. I do tell him off when he's naughty but I try to be fair. It's always on my mind, though, that our discussions might go straight back to his mum.*
>
> NIKKI, STEPMUM FOR ONE YEAR TO STEPSON
> AGED FOUR

It's only natural to want to be liked and for people to recognise you're doing a good job. This reaction is especially common in new stepmothers. As you grow in confidence, you realise that you are in control in your house. You and your partner make the rules and you and your partner are entitled to make sure the children stick to them. With your partner's support, you should eventually gain confidence in your abilities as a parent and learn not to worry about what your stepchildren say about you. The chances are, it's all good anyway!

DEALING WITH JEALOUSY

Jealousy is related to feelings of insecurity, fear and anxiety of losing a relationship or love, and can be a serious hazard to stepfamilies. It's common for both adults and children in a stepfamily to feel jealous at times. Stepchildren may feel jealous of their new step-parent whom they see as 'taking away' their parent. They may also see the step-parent as 'competition' in terms of both time and affection for their parent. Step-parents on the other hand may feel like outsiders to the previous family unit and feel jealous, not only of their partner's relationship with his children but the enduring relationship with the ex. They may find themselves comparing themselves to the ex – such as in the way they look after their stepchildren or even the way they cook, to convince themselves how much 'better' at these things they are and thus feel more secure in their relationship with their partner. Secure people seldom feel jealous. They may feel envious or resentful, but if they are secure in their relationship, they'll rarely feel jealous.

If you find the green-eyed monster is rearing its head in your relationship, then it's time to take a look at the reasons behind it. If you're still struggling with finding your voice within the family, or feeling a bit low on confidence, it's all too easy to let negative thoughts creep into your head.

Tips to avoid the jealousy trap

➤ *Be honest with yourself.* Why do you feel the way you do? Is it because someone you love was once close to this person and that intimidates you, or perhaps it's because they share children together, something which your relationship doesn't have yet? Try not to dwell on things that you can't change. Learn to accept the past and enjoy the present.

➤ *Give yourself a reality check.* Take a look at the things that trigger your jealousy. What evidence do you have that your relationship is in danger? Is your behaviour actually making the situation worse?

➤ *Use positive reinforcement.* When you start feeling twinges of jealousy remind yourself that your partner has chosen to be with you. Their relationship with their ex may be enduring because of their children but their life is with you. Their relationship with their ex is one of necessity, not choice. If your jealousy is related to your stepchildren you need to recognise that these are two fundamentally different relationships and this should complement – not compete for – affection.

➤ *Seek reassurance.* If you're really struggling to deal with your feelings don't be afraid to ask your partner for reassurance and help in overcoming the problem.

Dwelling on negative thoughts about your partner's ex will only feed any jealousy you might feel. Feeling jealous is a behaviour that we learn so we need to find a way of changing the thought processes that produce the jealous feelings. The best way of achieving this is by recognising your own strengths. Rather than comparing yourself to your partner's ex, focus on how good your relationship is and how everyone individually benefits from that – including your stepchildren. Take a proactive approach. Each time you have a jealous thought, work out what the catalyst was and counter it with a positive one. So rather than 'Oh, he's talking to her again. It will remind him of how close they once were. I'm convinced she still loves him...' better to think 'Of course they need to talk, it will make things easier for the children. Their relationship was over a long time ago. I'm really proud of the new family unit we've created together'.

If you find yourself secretly comparing yourself to his ex, stop! It's just not good for you.

I recently spoke to Lara who had been a stepmum for two years and had really struggled in controlling her jealousy over her partner's ex. Although she had tried to tell herself she was being unreasonable, every time her partner phoned his ex or went to see her to pick up the children, she found herself wondering what they were talking about and whether they still had feelings for each other. Her mind was working overtime but she had no evidence to think anything was wrong at all. Her relationship with her partner was fine but she knew she had to try and control her jealousy – it was making her irritable and angry over the slightest thing, which wasn't good for her or her partner. She eventually – and embarrassingly – told her partner how she felt. He was really surprised that she had felt the way she had and reassured her that he was committed to their relationship. While he still had to see his ex he made sure that he was much more open with his partner in telling her the arrangements they'd agreed, so that she didn't feel so excluded. Over the next few weeks and months Lara found that she was thinking about her partner's ex less and less and her feelings of jealousy towards her had pretty much gone altogether.

Jealousy in small doses can be a good thing for a relationship. It reminds us not to take each other for granted and heightens our feelings of love towards our partner. But when it's intense or irrational it's time to take action and stop it destroying your relationship.

'CONTROLLING' THE CONTROL

One of the real bugbears of stepmothers is the perceived 'control' exerted by their partner's exes.

The ex-wife always has that control, you know whether it's nine o'clock on Saturday morning when she rings up asking to talk to the children, or giving instructions on what they should wear if it's cold. You know they're always there pulling the strings.

SHONA, STEPMUM FOR TWO YEARS TO STEPSON
AGED FIVE

I'm always being given orders...you're not allowed to do this, they're my children, you can't pick them up from school...the ex-wife dictates everything I'm allowed to do with my stepchildren.

RUTH, STEPMUM FOR ONE YEAR TO TWO STEPCHILDREN
AGED FIVE AND NINE

It can be difficult trying to build a new stepfamily with constant interruptions, instructions and commands from an anxious ex but the key is firstly in understanding the causes behind the intrusions and secondly to learn to control the controller.

There are three fundamental reasons why ex-partners try and interfere with you and your partner's relationship with their children. In order to control their interference you need to work out which of these applies in your case.

You may feel that you're dealing with the *jealous ex.* They haven't come to terms with the end of their relationship and don't want to see their ex getting on with his life. They'll do anything to make your life harder because they're still hurting and they want you to feel the same pain. They probably don't feel like they have a lot of control in their life any more but what little they do have they are intent on using.

But before you rush to put your partner's ex in this category, make sure they really are acting out of malice. They could be the *overanxious ex.* This ex can't bear the thought of her children being looked after by anyone other than her. She believes that only *she* knows what's best for her children. She worries from the moment they leave her and she just *has* to ring to check they're surviving without her. She can't help how she feels and doesn't even recognise that she is overanxious. She believes she's just being protective of her children.

Or maybe you have the *lonely ex*. Your partner's ex may simply be lonely and what you perceive as control is actually just a symptom of her loneliness. When her children visit you and your partner she's left on her own. Her life revolves around her children and, whether by choice or circumstance, she has no one special in her life. She rings her children because she's missing them – not to be a nuisance to you. Her children are pretty much her life so when they're not around she's at a loss what to do with herself and just waits for them to return.

Once you've decided which 'ex' you have, it's simply a matter of controlling the symptoms. For those with the jealous ex you'll need to work with your partner to limit the effect on your stepfamily. This ex typically tries to throw her weight around by dictating what you can and can't do. The trick here is for you and your partner to choose your fights. Work out what's important to you. If the ex doesn't want you collecting the children from school but you can't anyway as you work, there's no point in making a big deal about it. But if, for example, it makes sense for you to pick them up because your partner is working then it's important that you find a solution. While it's easy to become angry at this type of situation it's only by approaching the issue in a calm way that you're likely to find a compromise.

Here are two possible scenarios:

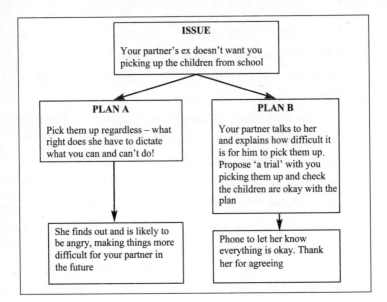

While 'Plan A' is the most obvious route, the chances are it will only lead to more animosity within the relationship over time. The ex will feel that her views are ignored. If she is intent on making your lives harder she may even stop the children from visiting as a form of punishment or initiate more rules regarding contact. 'Plan B' allows her to retain the control but makes it harder for her to refuse to work together on a compromise. By adopting a more conciliatory approach, she will find it harder to be so aggressive. Try and avoid fanning the flames any more than necessary. These women generally want a battle. By engaging you in their war they know they're 'winning'. By avoiding getting drawn into the conflict you can reduce the tension. It may take time but be patient. Not only will you find life getting easier, with fewer arguments, you can take pride in the fact you've adopted 'the higher ground' and not been drawn into fruitless battles.

On the other hand, anxious or lonely exes need reassurance. If you find they're constantly phoning to check on the children, try pre-empting the calls so that they're on your terms and explain that as you plan on being out for most of the weekend you thought they might appreciate a call from their children before you leave. If calls are becoming a real issue you need to make sure your partner talks to his ex about it. He needs to explain that while the odd call isn't a problem he would appreciate it if they didn't call so often. Reassure anxious exes that they will, of course, be contacted in the unlikely event that there is a problem. Lonely exes just need more time to get used to their own company and hopefully in time find things to do that don't involve the children. In the meantime, it's just a case of reassuring them.

As both a biological mother (whose children also have a stepmother) and a stepmother, I've spent some time pondering the difficulties between stepmothers and biological mothers. I've waved off my two children many times as they've spent time with their father and his new wife. I've listened to stories about what a good cook she is and what fun they've had. And I've tried my hardest not to criticise. As they leave me I tell them to have a great time and when they come back I show an interest (healthy I hope!) in what they've done. I'm convinced that I'm not the only mother who does this. I don't think we're all monsters.

While there are some things that you can consciously do as a biological mother to affect things in the stepfamily household, such as contacting your children excessively when they are with their father, or imposing rigid rules, such as demanding that the children are returned for specific times, most mothers don't consciously set out to cause problems. They may create them without knowing – sometimes just by their very existence. But most women, once they've come to terms with the end of their relationship, want to move on with their life.

It's important to hold on to this view. While some exes no doubt try and makes things hard for the stepmothers, whether out of malice, jealousy or loneliness, the majority of exes are more interested in getting on with their lives. Clearly they need to maintain a relationship with their children's father but this is purely for practical purposes. Concentrate on things that are in your control rather than things you can do nothing about. As always, talk to your partner about the things that worry you and try and find compromises. Once you've learned to accept that your partner's ex will always be part of your lives you're ready to move on and become the happy stepmum you want to be.

DIFFERENT VALUES, DIFFERENT MORALS?

If I had a pound for every time a stepmother has told me how difficult their partner's ex is I'd be very well off! Often, women tell me that they struggle to understand their stepchildren's mother and feel that she lives by inferior standards and values. As one stepmother told me:

> *Katie's mother is a complete sham. She should be ashamed of the way she behaves. She is a hopeless mother. We're the ones who show Katie how to*

behave, to say please and thank you. To eat properly at the table and generally have good manners. Her mother just doesn't seem to care.

KAREN, STEPMUM FOR THREE YEARS TO STEPDAUGHTER AGED SEVEN

While some mothers probably do behave in this way and are pretty poor at parenting, the chances are that most exes are the same as everyone else. We all bumble along in the best way we can, learning from our mistakes and bringing up our children to know right from wrong. Whether you like it or not, if your stepchildren spend time with their mother and with you and your partner, you're all in some way sharing the parenting responsibilities of the children. There are things that you will undoubtedly do better with your stepchildren than their mother but, likewise, there will be things she does better than you. You can't change the way your stepchildren behave when they're with their mother – but you can, for example, instil rules and good manners in your home. We all have different strengths and if we use them to help our children and stepchildren in the best way we can, they can benefit from having an extra parent to help them.

OUT OF FAVOUR WITH THE IN-LAWS

Some stepmothers find that they seem to be 'competing' for attention from their in-laws with their partner's ex, with their in-laws maintaining contact with the ex despite the breakdown of the relationship. One stepmother, Rose, told me that every year, her partner's ex had a Christmas card made of a photo of herself and her children, which she then sent to all their friends and relations. Whenever Rose visited her partner's relations she found herself having to deal with the ex's family Christmas card and photo. For the first two years, Rose found herself getting really upset over the 'family' Christmas card. However, over time she learned to accept it for what it was. Her partner's ex would always have a place in the family – but that didn't have to exclude Rose.

Often, the relationship between the ex and the in-laws is maintained as the in-laws want to keep strong links with their grandchildren. This enduring relationship can result in the stepmother feeling left out and very much 'second best'. If you find yourself in this situation you need to ask yourself whether your in-laws know that their actions are hurting you. The chances are they haven't considered your feelings and are just intent on not harming their own chances of maintaining their relationships with their grandchildren. Perhaps your partner could talk to them to explain how you feel? Perhaps they could see more of their grandchildren with you and your partner instead? Or maybe your in-laws haven't had time to come to terms with the relationship ending and want to support their ex-daughter-in-law through the transition. This set of relationships can become very complicated. If it's causing problems in your family it's worth spending some time in understanding the causes. Ask yourself the following questions:

➤ *What is the real problem*? Perhaps your in-laws make you feel unwelcome when you visit, or they constantly talk about your partner's ex, or maybe they only see your stepchildren when they're with their mother and not you and your partner.

➤ *What needs to change*? What would make things better for you? It may be that you would like to encourage your in-laws to visit you and your partner more so that they can see their grandchildren with you, or it might be that you want them to try and make you feel more welcome in the family.

➤ *Is this reasonable*? Before you try to instigate any changes make sure you and your partner ask yourselves if you're being reasonable. So, for example, it's unreasonable to expect your in-laws to stop seeing the ex if they have always had a good relationship with her, but it is reasonable to explain to them that while you understand they have that relationship you also want to get to know them better.

While you often need the help of your in-laws to improve your relationship with them, sometimes you can change things by simply shifting your mindset. You need to stop worrying about the relationship your in-laws have with your partner's ex and concentrate on developing your own relationship with them. Over time your in-laws will start to see you and your partner as a family. It's unimportant whether they see your partner's ex as well.

DEALING WITH ISSUES OVER FINANCE

Money can be one of the most contentious issues in step-families, as your partner may be expected to contribute to the running costs of his ex's household. This can cause financial hardship in the new stepfamily and lead to conflict between the couple. This conflict may arise because the step-mother feels the payments are unfair in some way or in more subtle ways, such as preventing them starting a family because they can't afford to.

The rules in the UK regarding maintenance are some-what confusing to say the least. The onus, however, is firmly placed on the 'non-residential' parent to provide funds for their children that are given to the residential parent. In some cases they are also required to provide maintenance for their partner. The agreed level of funding is more arbitrary and can either be agreed informally between the couple or via the courts or the Child Support Agency (CSA).

While the majority of stepmothers agree that their partners should support their children, the level of payments is often a source of conflict. What can have seemed fair at the time of the separation can seem unfair if circumstances change, such as the ex-partner moving in with a new partner or starting a better-paid job. This happened to Gill.

I have always understood that maintenance has to be paid for the stepchildren and it shows how responsible our other halves are. He signed into a contract before I met him that was obviously overstretching his budget given that he had to pay for his own place. Eventually, after a lot of expense on his behalf via solicitor bills, CSA rates were agreed. However, CSA rules depend on how much he earns only, not taking into account that I was not earning due to being pregnant and that his ex is in a well-paid job and living with her partner. This left us significantly worse off. They have had three long-haul holidays in two years, the kids have every new toy going and are generally spoiled rotten. In contrast, we have had no holidays in that time and are struggling to make ends meet. CSA rules also reduce payment for the number of nights stayed with their dad and the ex actively discouraged the kids from staying overnight so she would get more money. I feel this has caused so much stress in our relationship.

GILL, STEPMUM FOR FOUR YEARS TO TWO STEPCHILDREN AGED 12 AND 14, MUM TO BABY SON

In Gill's case, while their income had reduced, her partner's ex had formed a new relationship and was clearly significantly better off. While Gill and her partner could have asked the CSA to review their situation, it's not always straightforward and maintenance can remain a thorny issue in many step-families. The harsh facts are that when a couple separate, each person will have less disposable income after the split than before. Consequently both parties can end up feeling aggrieved.

If maintenance has been agreed and is unlikely to change then it's time to move on. Dwelling on things that are outside your control is only going to increase your stress and ultimately lead to more difficulties in your relationship, as your partner is caught between a rock and a hard place.

Rather than focus on what you haven't got, focus on what you have. Okay, you might have to budget but so do most people. If you feel the lack of finances is limiting your choices – such as whether you can consider having a child together or moving to a bigger house for all the children – talk to your partner about your options. Try and find a compromise that you can both live with. For example, if your house is really too small for your family but you can't afford to move, perhaps you can agree to review things in a year when finances might be clearer. In the meantime take the opportunity to enjoy your time as a couple when your stepchildren aren't around.

WHEN THE BIOLOGICAL MOTHER HAS DIED

Historically, stepfamilies were generally created after the death of one of the biological parents, when the surviving parent remarried; nowadays it's much more common for stepfamilies to be created following a divorce or separation. That said, there *are* obviously stepfamilies where the biological mother has died and the onerous task of bringing up the children resides with the biological father and his new partner. My research suggested that about 5 per cent of all stepmothers are looking after children whose mother has died.

Some stepmothers believe that things would be easier for them if their stepchildren's mother had died, making their lives less complicated and more like a traditional nuclear family. While that may be the case from their perspective, it's certainly not for their stepchildren. Coming into a family where your partner has been widowed and your stepchildren have lost a mother is incredibly hard to cope with. The death of a partner and parent destroys the world that existed for the family and it can be extremely difficult for a stepmother to fill the void left by the mother and live up to a reputation that can't ever be equalled. It's very hard to criticise someone who is no longer around to defend themselves and, as time goes by, people have the tendency to remember only the good things about someone, rarely the bad, and consequently you're left trying to live up to the perfect mother. Add the fact that the children, and probably your partner to a certain extent, are still mourning their mother and partner, it's likely to be a tough job. However, although you have to navigate through these difficulties early on in your relationship, the chances are that things will improve eventually as everyone comes to term with their losses and begins to bond in the new family.

In the meantime it's important that you concentrate on creating a supporting and secure family environment, with a sense of belonging for everyone. Try not to immediately assume the disciplining role: leave that to your partner as you slowly build the trust and respect of your stepchildren. Give them time to talk about their mother when they want to, without making them feel guilty. They need to understand that you are not there to replace their mother but are there to help them and look after them. As Jan said:

Adam was 12 when I came into his life and he was clearly really missing his mum. She'd died two years earlier and he was very quiet and withdrawn. I tried to give him time to get used to me. I concentrated on getting to know him and building his trust. Gradually over the next couple of years he came out of himself, he's come on leaps and bounds at school. He's a real leader now and very confident in himself. He's never really spoken much about his mum though. I think he just wants to remember the good times and there are always photos of her around the home. I think he feels I am a mum to him – just not his special mum. But he knows I'll always be there for him.

JAN, STEPMUM FOR SEVEN YEARS TO ADAM AGED 19, MUM TO TWO DAUGHTERS AGED 28 AND 25

As with all stepfamily types, living in a stepfamily where a biological parent has died has different challenges. It's not necessarily easier – or harder. Just different. Here are some things to consider.

1. Give your partner and his children space and time to grieve.
2. Encourage them to display photos and reminders of their biological mother in the home.
3. Be sensitive to their needs. Encourage them to talk about her if they want but also respect their need for privacy.
4. Keep reassuring the children that you are not replacing their mum, but that you care for them and will always be there for them.
5. Keep some of their family traditions, but don't be afraid to change some and introduce new ones to develop your own family identity.
6. Don't feel you have to do things the same way as your predecessor, but never criticise her.

7. Welcome your stepchildren's maternal grandparents and close family into your family and encourage them to visit or call.

Above all, just try and be sensitive to the losses of the rest of your immediate family. Although your stepchildren's mother will always be a hugely significant part of their lives and memories, you are filling an important gap in their lives and helping them grow up in a loving and caring family environment.

WHEN THE MOTHER IS ABSENT

Usually stepmums have to deal with situations where the biological mother is causing difficulties in your relationship by interfering, exerting control or simply making a nuisance of herself. However, in some cases, the biological mother chooses the opposite path and takes only a fleeting or non-existent interest in her children, leaving the stepmother to take over. Often the stepmother has no choice in the matter and is left literally 'holding the baby'. This can be difficult to deal with, both for the stepmother and the children who have been 'abandoned' by their mother.

Clara had been married to her husband for five years. They had a young son together and they also looked after Clara's stepson who was nine years old. Although he saw his mother from time to time they had no regular meetings and she played no real part in his upbringing or had any interest in his life. Clara had developed a close bond with her stepson and looked after him in the same way as her own son. Although she felt she loved them both differently, she had a strong attachment to him nevertheless. However, she was desperately concerned that over time he would start to question why his own mother didn't want anything to do with him, especially as he saw what a close bond Clara had developed with her son. He had started to ask her difficult questions about his mother and Clara was at a loss to know what to say to him to reassure him, as she couldn't understand why his mother had chosen to behave in the way she had.

While it may seem the perfect solution for stepmothers in not having to deal on a daily basis with an interfering ex, for the stepchildren the lack of the physical presence of their mother does not mean 'out of sight, out of mind'. The children are likely to feel rejected or even wonder what they've done to cause their mother to leave. They may blame their stepmother in some way for replacing their mother. It can also leave them unable to trust those that care for them, wondering if they too are going to leave. So although from the stepmother's view, an absent mother can seem to have certain advantages, these are less clear cut from the children's perspective and may lead to more behavioural problems as they struggle to accept the situation.

If you find yourself in this situation it's important to reassure your stepchildren that they are not in any way to blame for it. Resist the urge to talk negatively about the absent parent in front of your stepchildren – despite your own views.

Depending on the age of your stepchildren, answer any questions they have about their absent parent as honestly as you can, but sensitively. So if, for example, they ask when their mum is coming back, don't lie if you don't know. Just explain that you aren't sure but that you and their father are still here for them and will always look after them. Focus on building trust with your stepchildren. Be prepared to be patient and give them time to adjust to the changes in the family. Try and find activities that you can do together so that they can start to feel more secure and part of the new family unit.

Practical tips for dealing with the ex-factor

If you are to truly move on in your relationship with your partner and stepchildren it's important to recognise the issues you have with your stepchildren's mother and put together an action plan to address the problems.

➤ Learn to accept that your partner's ex is part of your extended family. She will always be a presence in your lives because of the children.

➤ Allow your stepchildren to talk positively about *both* their biological parents. Children need to believe the best about their mother and father.

➤ Conceal any negative views you may have about your partner's ex from the children in your family. If you need to let off steam do it in private with your partner.

➤ When you're feeling isolated from the biological family, remember that the ex suffers as well. When the stepchildren are with you, you are in charge of her children. This can cause her to feel equally isolated.

➤ Accept that some things are out of your control – such as the behaviour of your partner's ex or what she tells your stepchildren. Rise above this and focus on what you *can* control.

➤ Let your actions speak for themselves. Don't worry about what your stepchildren might say to their mother about you. Just behave in the way you feel is fair and consistent.

➤ Don't be jealous of the past. Concentrate on the here and now. Your partner has chosen to spend his life with you.

➤ If your partner's ex is making your life a misery and nothing seems to work, don't give up. Disarm them with reason – and a smile. The saying 'one hand clapping' comes to mind here. You can't clap with one hand and you can't argue with yourself. If she's intent on creating arguments and problems don't let her! Keep smiling through gritted teeth!

Don't forget that eventually things will improve. The first two years of a relationship are the most difficult, where everyone involved is adapting to their new lives. You may not like your partner's ex or you may feel she treated your partner badly but she is, and will always be, your stepchildren's mother. You need to accept that she has an important part to play in their lives so make an effort to treat her with respect, which she will hopefully return.

I was fed up with being left out of all the decisions regarding my stepdaughter. I really cared for her but didn't seem to have a say in anything. Her mother would always try and create this biological family unit, with me as the outsider. As my stepdaughter's birthday was approaching I rang her up out of the blue. Knowing that she worked full-time and didn't have a lot of free time, I offered to help arrange the party. I was pregnant at the time and not working so I had time on my hands. I made it clear I wanted to help and not take over and while she was a little wary at first, we jointly organised the party and it was a real success. I wouldn't say that we are the greatest of friends or anything, but she knows now that I care for her daughter and she trusts me to do the right things for her when she's with us.

CLAIRE, STEPMUM FOR THREE YEARS TO STEPDAUGHTER
AGED EIGHT

Conclusion: Putting It All into 'Practise'

When I started writing this book my aim was to highlight the most common problems that face stepfamilies and provide you with the tools to tackle these problems effectively. As a new stepmum myself 10 years ago, I was completely oblivious to the challenges that lay ahead. I just assumed that because I loved my partner and he loved me, the rest would fall into place. Unsurprisingly, this wasn't the case. But as I began researching stepfamily behaviour I realised that the problems we faced as a new stepfamily and the way I felt as a stepmum were common and perfectly normal. Through my research and by speaking to stepmums in similar positions I identified some of the most common problem areas. It's my belief that if you can focus on these areas you can make a difference to your stepfamily.

Partnership

You and your partner are the foundation of your new family and it's vital that your relationship together is strong. You need to work together to develop the household rules and your individual roles in the family. If you don't want to be responsible for disciplining your stepchildren then your partner needs to know, or if your partner expects you to be a replacement mum he needs to make sure that that's something you're prepared to be. Take time to talk about your expectations and set realistic goals. Work at the way you communicate together. When we're frustrated or angry it's often easier to talk but forget to listen to the other person. Remember, there are always two sides to everything and you owe it to your partner and your relationship to take time to listen. Above all, make time for your partner so that you can rely on each other when you're feeling low. Find time away from the children – whether it's a sneaky weekend away in the country or a candlelit meal at home when the children are in bed – make time for just the two of you so that you're ready to take on the world together.

Resentment

While we're often not proud of it, resentment is a common feeling for stepmums. When it comes to looking after our stepchildren we're often expected to take on board the majority of practical jobs. Whether it's washing their clothes, cooking their meals or cleaning their rooms, the buck generally stops with us. And then there's the emotional impact, such as coming to terms with being somehow different from biological families, and even perhaps the loss of independence or the impact on your social life. The changes that life in a stepfamily can bring can also lead to building resentment, which can be directed at your partner or your stepchildren. It's important to recognise if you're suffering from resentment and try and restore some balance in your life. It's often easy to count up the negatives while you skip over all the positives, so take time to balance the 'costs and rewards' in your family. Your stepchildren may not thank you for making their bed or cooking their favourite meal but often a hug or a smile can more than make up for it. Following Mother's Day recently I received an email from a stepmum. She couldn't wait to tell me that she'd had the best day ever. Her stepdaughter had sent her a card and written inside '*Thank you for being mine. You are the best stepmum there could ever possibly be*'. Somehow that made all the years of heartache worth it.

Ambiguity

One of the main reasons being a stepmum is so hard is the fact that there are no role models for us to follow. We're not quite sure what we're supposed to do so we just muddle along doing our best, which can lead to ever-increasing frustration and helplessness. It's important that you take time to work out what you want your role to be within your family. Do you want to be involved in day-to-day decisions or do you want to take more of a back seat and support your partner? It matters more that you both agree on your role than the actual role. As long as you're both clear how you want things to work in your family, it's likely to work. It's only when there's confusion that problems arise.

Coping

People cope with things in different ways. And while most of these coping styles are effective, there are some that are more likely to prolong the problem and not solve it. If you feel that you generally avoid things and hide in the hope that things will 'sort themselves out' or simply go away, it's probably not a good long-term strategy for happiness. Whether it's relying on advice from friends or simply learning to accept the situation, try and find a way of coping for you that ultimately leads to less stress and anxiety.

Time

As a stepmum you need to be patient and give everyone time to get used to the changes – both within your stepfamily and in the wider family and friends. Relationships take time to build and for everyone to really get to know one another. It's generally recognised that the first two years are the most difficult for stepfamilies, with things generally calming down after this period. However, some stepmums have told me that their experiences were different to this with a kind of prolonged honeymoon period, where the first two years were fantastic, followed by several years of turmoil. So whether your problems start on day 1 or a little later, forewarned is forearmed. Try not to have unrealistic expectations about your family. Building a new family in any situation is a big challenge, but a hugely rewarding one, and one that's going to take time. So when things are difficult remind yourself that Rome wasn't built in a day. Take a deep breath and work out how you're going to tackle the latest problem.

Integration

If your stepfamily is going to work, you need to work hard at giving it its own identity, where all its members have a sense of belonging. When you bring a stepfamily together, you're merging two different families, each with their own traditions and memories. While it's important not to discard everything from the past and try and erase previous memories, it's important that you start building your own unique family traditions and memories. Whether it's the way you celebrate Christmas, or the way you always eat Sunday dinner together as a family, make sure you include everyone to make them feel part of your family. If you don't act as a family then others won't see you as a family and treat you that way. Occasionally, when I've been on holiday with my family, people that we've met on our travels, either on the aeroplane or sitting on the beach, have told me what a lovely family I have and I'm so proud – not that they think we're a 'normal' family but that there's no difference between us and a family with just biological children. So if you're finding it hard to include your stepchildren in your definition of 'family' think about what might be stopping you. Take time to work with your partner and the children to set household rules so that everyone's included and pulls their weight. And don't forget that other family members and friends will need a bit of guidance and help as well to understand how you want things to work!

Support

Everyone needs help from time to time, whether it's advice or simply a shoulder to cry on when things are difficult. If we can't turn to anyone for that support, though, it's easy to let things get on top of us and we can become more and more desolate and depressed. While we need our partner's support – and this is often the first person we turn to when we need help – it's equally important that there are other people we can rely on, such as our family and friends, who might be able to offer a different perspective or perhaps just listen without trying to fix a problem. If you find that you haven't got as much support as you need, whether that's from your in-laws, your friends or even your partner, take steps to rectify the situation. Perhaps your in-laws are struggling to accept the changes and feel torn between supporting your partner's ex and you, or perhaps you feel that your friends don't understand your problems any more. Think about what you'd like to change and work out how you could improve things, so that you give yourself the cushion of support you need in times of crisis.

Ex-factor

The presence of the ex is recognised to be one of the major causes of anxiety for many stepmums. Whether it's the ongoing financial commitment and the subsequent impact on your resources, the way she looks after the children, or her enduring relationship with the in-laws, the ex is a constant presence in the lives of stepmothers. But while there are exes whose main mission is to cause difficulties for the new stepfamily out of bitterness or jealousy, the majority simply want to get on with their lives. If you find that you're struggling to deal with your feelings towards your partner's ex, work out why you feel so angry or stressed. Use the tips in Chapter 8 to help you cope with your feelings. And try and stand in her shoes – work out why she's behaving the way she is: is she simply jealous, or is it anxiety or loneliness which drive her behaviour? Try and understand the causes for why she behaves the way she does and then work with your partner to put a plan together to help reduce the impact the ex has on your lives.

While there are lots of difficulties facing stepfamilies it's important to put everything in perspective. All couples and all families face problems – all the time. Stepfamilies aren't unique, but they do have unique problems. Although it's important to recognise issues in your family it's equally important not to get obsessed by them. Take a moment every day to count your blessings. In today's fast-moving world it's easy to forget how much we have got to be grateful for, whether it's a loving relationship with our partner, supportive family and friends, happy and healthy children or a lovely home. Remember, life's never perfect but we can strive to make it as good as we possibly can.

ADVICE FROM OTHER STEPMUMS

It's fine to listen to the 'experts' but ultimately the best way we can learn is through talking to others who have been through the same experiences. As you'll see from the words of the stepmums below, the same problems crop up time and time again – the importance of setting your boundaries and rules, the support of your partner, the need for good communication, realistic expectations and the power of time. These are the things that you need to make sure you have in place if you're to improve things in your stepfamily. But above all, don't beat yourself up or set yourself unrealistic goals. Take things a day at a time and eventually you will become that happy stepmum you deserve to be.

Make sure you love your husband enough to do this, because if I didn't love my husband enough I couldn't do it. Also make sure you set boundaries before you start. Your husband needs to be totally supportive of the way you look after the children, and you must have great communication or it won't work. And finally, be prepared to give up an awful lot emotionally and timewise.

CARA, STEPMUM FOR FIVE YEARS TO THREE STEPCHILDREN
AGED FROM 10 TO 15

Don't try and be anything other than just a grown-up friend to your stepchildren. Make sure you set the parameters with your partner, say what you're prepared to do and what you're not. I didn't do that and there were no boundaries. I ended up getting involved in everything and felt put upon. I should have said, no, this is not my child, you need to get involved and take her out. So, set out your expectations about what you are prepared to do from the beginning, outline it very clearly, have your parameters and limitations.

NICKY, STEPMUM FOR 11 YEARS TO 17-YEAR-OLD
STEPDAUGHTER

Be relaxed about things, try and enjoy your time with them and their company, have fun and don't try too hard because it can go wrong! Keep telling yourself it will get better over time.

MANDY, STEPMUM FOR SEVEN YEARS TO TWO STEPSONS
AGED 12 AND 14

Don't have any preconceived notions. Be yourself, be interested in the children and show them love and affection. Support each other. Children are really straightforward, especially boys, and they will respond if you show them affection and be interested in what they're doing.

GEMMA, STEPMUM FOR FIVE YEARS TO STEPSONS
AGED 8 AND 11

Over the past 10 years, my husband and I have muddled through and somehow emerged relatively unscathed on the other side. Our journey has at times been really hard – but overall it's been a fantastic experience and I'm extremely proud of my stepfamily and *all* the children in it. I hope you can gain the confidence from this book to do the same and become a truly happy stepmum.

Useful Resources

Happy Steps
www.happysteps.co.uk
A website developed and managed by Dr Lisa Doodson, dedicated to providing support for stepfamilies. Includes helpful articles on step-parenting together with details on step-parenting courses, self-help courses and one-to-one coaching.

Family and Parenting Institute
www.familyandparenting.org.uk
The Family and Parenting Institute is a centre of expertise on families and parenting in the UK. Its website offers advice and support to all families – including stepfamilies.

Relate
Tel: 0300 100 1234
www.relate.org.uk
An established charity that aims to support and help couples and families through a varied counselling service. Relate offers advice, relationship counselling, sex therapy, work-shops, mediation, consultation and support face-to-face, by phone and through their website.

Stepfamily Scotland
Tel: 0845 122 8655
www.stepfamilyscotland.org.uk
A national charity aimed at offering advice and support for stepfamilies.

Parentline plus

Tel: 0808 800 2222

www.parentlineplus.org.uk

A national charity that works with parents, providing support and advice on all aspects of family life.

One Up Magazine

www.oneupmagazine.co.uk

An independent online magazine aimed at offering support and advice for single parents and stepfamilies.

Care for the Family

www.careforthefamily.org.uk

A national charity promoting family life and offering help to those who have experienced family breakdown.

The British Second Wives Club

www.thebritishsecondwivesclub.co.uk

An independent website offering advice and friendship for second wives and stepmothers.

Childless Stepmums

www.childlessstepmums.co.uk

An online support group aimed predominantly at women who become stepmothers and don't have children of their own.

Index

Also available from Vermilion

Divas & Dictators

By Charlie Taylor

Supermarket tantrums? Insufferable car journeys? Sibling in-fighting? Sound familiar?

Behavioural expert Charlie Taylor has the answers in this practical handbook, which is full of simple, effective techniques for improving your child's behaviour.

Focusing predominately on the under-fives, Charlie Taylor's straight-talking, no-nonsense approach guides you away from knee-jerk parenting towards a more proactive and positive relationship with your child. With particular emphasis on the power of praise, and planning in advance for behaviour hotspots, every parent can break the miserable pattern of confrontation and nagging and bring harmony to their household.

£10.99   ISBN 9780091923853

Order this title direct from www.rbooks.co.uk